WHY
GIVE?

WHY GIVE?

40 Days — From Getting to Giving

John F. DeVries

Grand Rapids, Michigan
info@missionindia.org

Mission India
PO Box 141312
Grand Rapids, Michigan 49514-1312
info@missionindia.org
www.missionindia.org

WHY GIVE?
© 2009 by John F. DeVries

ISBN 978-0-9788551-3-0

First Printing, 2009

2 3 4 5 6 7 Printing/Year 14 13 12 11 10

Cover photo courtesy of iStockphoto
Background photo courtesy of Stock Exchange / Dora Pete
Cover design by Kelly Robinson / www.kropmark.com

"Because He Lives" (pp. 105–106), lyric by Gloria Gaither
and William J. Gaither, music by William J. Gaither.
Copyright © 1971, 1979 bt William J. Gaither.

Unless otherwise noted, Scripture quotations are taken from the
Holy Bible, New International Version®. Copyright © 1973, 1978,
1984 International Bible Society. Used by permission of Zondervan.
All rights reserved. Scripture quotations marked NLT are taken from
the Holy Bible. New Living Translation copyright © 1996 by Tyndale
Charitable Trust. Used by permission of Tyndale House Publishers.
Italics in Scripture are added by the author for emphasis.

Verses marked TLB are taken from *The Living Bible*, © 1971, Tyndale
House Publishers, Wheaton, IL 60189. Used by permission.

Scripture quotations marked NKJV are taken from the
New King James Version. Copyright © 1982 by Thomas
Nelson, Inc. Used by permission. All rights reserved.

*To the thousands of faithful friends who
through their prayers and sacrificial gifts
have become rivers of life to millions in India*

Dr. John DeVries is the founder of a Christian nonprofit organization called Mission India. You will notice frequent references to the people of India in this book. You will also sense his deep love for India and his intense desire to reach its people with the glorious news that Jesus Christ loves them. John invites you to visit the Mission India website at www.missionindia.org. Please contact us at (877) 644-6342 or info@missionindia.org if you would like to learn more about Mission India.

PO Box 141312
Grand Rapids, MI 49514-1312

Contents

Foreword

You have already asked yourself the question that is the title of this book. Every Christian believer who is making a serious effort to follow Jesus has asked it. John DeVries answers the question in ways that open the door to the paradoxical joy that follows biblical giving.

Before John and I became friends and colleagues, I heard him preach a "Mission Emphasis" sermon that helped me to think about giving in a new way. John has a way of telling stories that demand your attention, and John's story of the husband who claimed to love his wife but never gave her anything of value helped me to see the connection between my giving and my relationship to God.

John's message reminded me that "Why Give?" is a question that every single believer needs to answer. When I lived in the Philippines, I taught discipleship in an extremely poor rural congregation of new believers who were perpetually under-employed, whose children sometimes died of malnutrition, and whose daily income was not enough to buy the cup of coffee that many of us consume each morning. The question "Why should they give?" hit me in the face every Sunday morning: Did we really need to pass the offering plate to people whose children had not eaten a meal in two days?

Years later, I witnessed the joy of poor believers in India who had discovered the secret of sacrificial giving. The Mizo believers in Northeast India don't limit their giving to Sunday morning or to a measly ten percent of their meager incomes. They take every opportunity to give generously in every way imagin-able. They have so little and yet they give systematically and passionately. Why do they do this?

The book you are holding in your hand answers that question. Discovering these answers, you will also discover the mystery of God's grace. John shares many stories, from poor people and wealthy people, from India and North America, that will inspire and encourage you to participate in the marvelous grace of giving.

You might be tempted to read through the book quickly. I recommend that you consume only a few pages a day. Follow the 40-day schedule, answer the questions for reflection and discussion, and discover six weeks from today the joy that has surprised so many who have learned the holy pleasures of generous giving.

David Stravers, President
Mission India

Acknowledgements

I am deeply grateful to the many who have helped so much in the challenging task of preparing this book. A special thanks to:

- my wife for her daily counsel;
- Josh Visser, who rescued this project at the last minute;
- Lindsay Ackerman for her painstaking, patient work in final corrections and her excellent editing; and
- Brad Formsma, Bruce Cheadle, and Mike and Steve DeVries for their encouragement and suggestions.

I would like to list those whose generosity and joy have been such an inspiration through these years; but there are so many, and I am certain I would probably leave some out. So to all of you whose joyful, sacrificial giving through Mission India has been a channel of blessing to millions in India, I express my deepest gratitude.

Introduction

We are going to be together for the next forty days; that's five weeks, seven days a week, concluding with five days of review. In these next weeks, we will be studying and practicing the grace of giving. That may seem a lot of time to you. But should you have second thoughts about making this kind of commitment, remember—joy and giving are related proportionately. The more you give, the more you will rejoice. Giving produces joy.

Scrooge, that old miser in Charles Dickens' "A Christmas Carol," was a miserable old man until he learned how to give. By the end of the story, he is dancing and giggling through the village, having discovered the joy of giving. The purpose of this book is for you to find something very much like that joy. *Why Give?* seeks to increase your influence toward three kinds of joy: joy in heaven, joy in your heart, and joy in the lives of those who receive your gifts (and who in turn are enabled to give to others and start new cascading rivers of joy). I am confident it will be worth your time!

We Are Born Again to Be Rivers, Not Lakes

In the next six weeks you'll find new experiences of joy as you learn new lessons in giving. In the first week you will see a new way of understanding what it means to be born again; namely, being born again from the motionless existence of a pond to being a vital and active river. Spiritual rebirth is like going from the stagnation of the Dead Sea to the roaring power of a mighty river, filled with torrents of living water. The former absorbs all the water flowing into it, while a flowing stream delivers fresh water to all the living things along its banks. Which would you rather be? Which is more exciting? Are you living to get or living to give?

In the second week you will be introduced to what we as Christians give when we give our money, our time, and our concern to others. Are we giving merely our resources, or do we give something infinitely more? What does our river really deliver?

Through our giving we are bringing the seven infinite gifts of Christ: his presence, power, provision, perfection, resurrection, reign, and return. These seven gifts flow through every gift we give. Understanding what we are *really* giving as we give time and money and encouragement in Christ's name produces a new urgency, thrill, and excitement about giving. We always give these seven infinite gifts when we give to others in Jesus' name. When we consider what each of Christ's gifts is "worth" and what transforming power each has in the lives of those who are hopeless, we gain an entirely new understanding of the importance of Christian giving.

In week three we will see that our giving releases God to give.

Bring all the tithes into the storehouse so that there will be food enough in my Temple; if you do, I will open up the windows of heaven for you and pour out a blessing so great you won't have room enough to take it in! Try it! Let me prove it to you! (Malachi 3:10 TLB).

We will see that God never works with simple addition but always multiplies both the results of our gifts and the new resources needed to give even more. We give because our giving moves God to open the "windows [floodgates] of heaven." Our giving moves God to give things *he would not give if we did not give.* Not only will the impact of our giving be beyond our imagination, but the increase of our resources enabling us to give more will be beyond all expectation.

In the fourth week we will look at the power giving has to either degrade or dignify. We will see that giving in the name of Jesus is starting new rivers. Our gifts to others must have the primary purpose of enabling them to give. Our gifts must result in making them new "headwaters" of additional torrents of living water. Jesus taught us that the greatest gift we can give to another is to ask them for a gift! We must never think that the final result of giving is filling another person's need. It is so much more than that! It is enabling that person to fill the needs of someone else. We must always think multiplication not addition. Our giving must always enable and encourage others to give.

Finally, we will join "Scrooge" as he dances through his village at the end of the "Christmas Carol," laughing and singing for joy, for he has been delivered from his miserly misery and has discovered giving as the source of real joy. In a study of 2 Corinthians 8:1–7 we will discover seven wonderful dimensions of joy in giving. And in our five-day epilogue we will review the five principles of giving and encourage you to set up an "experimental" faith promise giving project.

Biblical Rivers

A river watering the garden flowed from Eden; from there it was separated into four headwaters. (Genesis 2:10)

Then the angel showed me the river of the water of life, as clear as crystal, flowing from the throne of God and of the Lamb down the middle of the great street of the city. On each side of the river stood the tree of life, bearing twelve crops of fruit, yielding its fruit every month. And the leaves of the tree are for the healing of the nations. (Revelation 22:1–2)

There are four possible ways we might answer the question, "Why give?" The first is that giving is mentioned some

2,500 times in the Bible. The next closest subject to be mentioned multiple times is mentioned only 500 times. I didn't count them all myself, but this is a well accepted number. It would seem safe to say that giving is among the most important subjects discussed in the Bible! We need to take giving seriously because the Bible does. It talks about giving more than any other subject!

That's fairly motivating, but there is even better motivation for giving. Joy and giving go together. Do you want to live the good life? Do you want to be happy? Start giving!

Charles Dickens captured that idea in his famous "A Christmas Carol." The central character, Scrooge, has become a synonym for miserliness and misery. Miserly people are miserable people. Yet by the end of "A Christmas Carol," Scrooge is transformed from an attitude of getting to one of giving, fostered through a series of visions on Christmas Eve. Now he is dancing through the village streets, giggling and laughing, as he discovers the joy of giving and lavishly spreads

Christmas gifts to all he meets.

Personal joy is a worthy motivation. Hebrews 12:2 tells us that it was the anticipation of the "joy set before him" that enabled Christ to give his life on Calvary's cross. Jesus was fortified on the cross by the anticipation of the eternal joy that would come through his sacrificial death. Joy and giving go together. Want more joy? Give more!

We will return to the subject of joy and giving many times. But let's move on to a third reason for giving, which I call the "Western reason." We give because we are created in God's image; and since he is a giving God we, as his image bearers, must also be generous people. To be in God's image means that we, like him, must naturally generous. I like this reason. But it is abstract and perhaps less accessible to some.

The final reason for giving, and the one we explore in this first week of meditations, also represents the "Eastern reason" for giving. Eastern people, including people who lived in Bible times, did not think so much in abstract concepts but rather in pictures taken from nature. They spoke in vivid, natural images. Jesus is called a Shepherd, a Rock, a Bright and Morning Star. They used images from nature to explain their religion. Western Christians tend to think in abstract concepts, while Eastern people emphasize concrete nature images.

Rivers are nature images, and the image of a river is the backbone of Scripture. The Bible opens with a river image, and the last chapter of the Bible closes with a river image. The river first appears in the creation story of Genesis 2:10, and the Bible concludes with the image of the river in Revelation 22:1, where heaven is pictured in terms of a river flowing through the center of the eternal city.

We are *born again to be a river through which the Spirit flows.* This definition of being born again to be a river is not well known, but we won't forget it once we hear it. To be born again is to be a river, not a pond, or a lake, or a Dead Sea. Ponds and lakes keep their water, but a river carries and gives its water. A river provides life wherever it flows. The heavenly river nurtures the tree of life, which stands on each side, bearing a monthly harvest of fruit along with healing leaves for the nation (Revelation 22:1-2). A river flows from Eden in anticipation of the river that will flow in heaven. Rivers are pictures of *giving Christians*. All who are born again are the rivers through which the Spirit flows from the time of creation to the final redemption (John 7:38-39).

So, we give because being born again is about living the good life—caring for what God's Word cares about, pursuing unbridled joy, desiring to be more like God, and being rivers of life for our stagnant and dead world!

REFLECTION AND DISCUSSION

1. What impressed you the most in this meditation?
2. What new ideas about God did you gain?
3. Be quiet and meditate. How is the Spirit telling you to apply these truths? Write down the ideas that come to mind. Share them and hold each other accountable to do them.

4. How does our giving provide life? Give examples.

God as a River

Fruit trees of all kinds will grow on both banks of the river. Their leaves will not wither, nor will their fruit fail. Every month they will bear, because the water from the sanctuary flows to them. Their fruit will serve for food and their leaves for healing. (Ezekiel 47:12)

Does that verse seem familiar? One of the concluding verses of the Bible, Revelation 22:2, first appears in the Old Testament in Ezekiel 47:12, which John echoes to describe his vision of God's new and eternal city.

Ezekiel's river vision is a picture of God, and indeed a river is a picture of the very nature of God. We have a choice between a river or pond when we think of God. Is God a river of giving, or is he a stagnant pond pulling everything into itself and keeping everything?

God is either a demanding, self-centered, denying God, as Satan led Adam and Eve to believe; or he is the epitome of generosity. The primary purpose of the first two chapters of the Bible is to show us the infinite generosity of a perfect God. It pictures torrents of life pouring from him.

God was giving, even in the command not to eat of the tree of life. The command was the greatest gift, the gift of an opportunity to freely give love and obedience and thus come into the full image of God. How could Adam and Eve believe that God limited them when he gave them everything, even the opportunity to choose to freely love him?

Satan tries to convince us that God is a "getting" God who restrains us, and that he is the God of the *no*, not the *yes*.

Now the serpent was more cunning than any beast of the field which the LORD God had made. And he said to

the woman, "Has God indeed said,
'You shall not eat of every tree in the
garden?'" (Genesis 3:1 NKJV)

He tricked Eve into believing that God
was not fair. Satan is still at it today, blind-
ing our eyes and tricking us into thinking
that God is a miserly God who is always
after our money. But it is Satan who is the
"stagnant, dead pond," always devoted to
getting. In order to selfishly have everything flow into him and thus gain the
world, he lies, saying that God is harsh,
demanding, and fearsome, when in reality those lies describe Satan and not God.
All of heaven is devoted to the "outward
flow" of a river, not the "inward flow" of
the Dead Sea; and because Satan chose
the "inward flow," he was permanently
removed from the joy of heaven's giving
and loving.

God is the opposite of an entity into
which everything flows. As the triune
God—Father, Son, and Holy Spirit—his
love flows outward through the three
persons of the Trinity. Even within his
inmost being the flow of love is outward.

God is a river of life, producing life and fruit. God created the entire world as a gift for Adam and Eve to be able to give as he gives.

The Garden of Eden was like a huge banquet table with every imaginable food heaped on it. There were candles in the middle, and God wisely said, "Don't eat the candles—they will make you sick; but you can eat everything else! But in commanding you to not eat the candles, I am giving you the greatest gift of all, the gift of being able to freely love me by the obedience you show me." Adam and Eve chose, however, to "eat the forbidden fruit"; and in doing that they chose to be a stagnant, lifeless Dead Sea, devoted to getting and not giving. Living to get, instead of living to give, results in sin and death.

They adopted Satan's principle that it is more important *to get than to give*. When we live to get, we separate ourselves by putting ourselves before all others. When we are devoted to getting, we are devoted to having everything flow into us.

Adam and Eve disregarded all that

God had given and concentrated only on the one thing he had denied them, not realizing that God's command to not eat of the tree was also a gift. That command opened the door to the greatest gift, the gift of being able to love God and give themselves through obedience, freely and without force.

Obeying God would have opened the floodgates of the rivers of life flowing from them. But they failed to trust that the command to not eat of the fruit of the tree was a gift opening the way to even greater joy. They failed to see that giving is the road to ultimate happiness. They believed Satan's lie that God is a demanding and deceitful God and that joy and happiness would only increase by obtaining what God had denied them.

God told Adam and Eve that if they disobeyed and ate the fruit of the Tree of the Knowledge of Good and Evil, the principle of getting would replace giving, and they would surely die. Concern for self first of all separates us from joy, from life, from growth. They would dry up like a stagnant pond. If the principle of getting governed their life, they would become like the Dead Sea — a sea that has only an inlet and no outlet, that holds everything and gives nothing.

God created us for the purpose of revealing his generosity. We are the primary recipients of God's gifts, not for the purpose of holding them, but for the purpose of becoming rivers of blessing to others. The creation story of the first chapter of Genesis is a revelation of the way God gives to man. All of creation was prepared as a massive gift for humans, enabling them in turn to be image bearers of God's generosity as they lovingly gave and cared for his creation.

In order to understand who we are, we need to understand who God is. If God is the ultimate picture of generous giving, then we must reflect that generosity, for we are created in his image and likeness. If God is a river, then being born again means we become rivers of giving.

REFLECTION AND DISCUSSION

1. What did you learn about God in this meditation?
2. What did you learn about yourself?
3. List major gifts that make up God's river of giving.
4. In what specific way will you apply this meditation to your life?

Gushing Torrents of Living Water

Whoever believes in me, as the Scripture has said, streams [torrents] of living water will flow from within him. (John 7:38)

It was the last day of the seven-day Feast of Tabernacles. Thousands gathered in the temple in Jerusalem. It was noisy. The crowd was excited. This was the big day! This was the day in which the priests acted out the vision of a stream flowing from the temple. It was a reenactment of the vision of Ezekiel, which always culminated in this the greatest of all feasts.

Dressed in their white robes, the

priests solemnly walked down to the pool of Siloam and filled their golden pitchers with the precious water. Up they came to the temple proper and poured out the water on the temple floor. They watched it trickle over the floor and out the south side of the temple, flowing past the altar.

And the crowd shouted with jubilation! It was a picture of the importance of the Jewish nation, for it was a picture of God dwelling in them and flowing out of them. They thought that the Jewish nation was to become the center of all nations. They were the important ones from whom God's blessings would flow.

The young rabbi, Jesus, just beginning his ministry, stood watching. He did not sit down to teach as did the typical rabbis. He stood. And then suddenly, with a loud voice, shouting to be heard above the rabble, he exclaimed, "Whoever believes in me, as the Scripture has said, [torrents] of living water will flow from within him" (John 7:38).

The crowd was struck dumb. What did he say? What blasphemy did he utter? How could this be? Of all of Christ's claims, even his claim to be divine and be able to forgive sins, none were so startling as the one he made this day in the temple at the very moment the priests poured the water on the floor! It was unimaginable to say that the temple was not the source of the river, but that everyone who believed in him would become a river!

The words Jesus spoke that day were prophetic. The generous Father, in Christ, has moved his temple from that stone building twenty kilometers above the Dead Sea in Jerusalem, into the heart of every believer! First Peter 2:5 says that we are living stones cemented together to become a "spiritual house" — God's temple. It is from within us, as we are filled with God's Holy Spirit, that torrents of living water gush out, transforming barren lives and landscapes with the life and love of God.

Christians give and give and give again because we are the fulfillment of the vision of Ezekiel. Jesus predicted that God would spread his temple over all the earth through scattering disciples everywhere. No nation, tribe, language, or people would be excepted (Revelation 7:9). God wants torrents of eternal life to flow to everyone everywhere; to all persons and families, villages and neighborhoods. He wants torrents and torrents of his blessings and resources to flow through us. That is why the central characteristic of being born again is the characteristic of giving.

A bishop of the Church of North India told me that he believed the primary sign of a person's faith in Christ was giving! He went on to say that he did not believe a person could be saved and be stingy at the same time. Salvation means that God's resources flow through us. Christians are the channels of God's blessings to their family, village, neighborhood, and nation. Becoming a disciple is like becoming a "leaky temple" out of which flows expanding streams of blessings. If we remain stingy, selfish, and unwilling to sacrifice, we are nonfunctioning disciples, and there can be no such thing! When we fail to give, we fail in the purpose for which God has created and redeemed us. To be created in God's image means that we demonstrate the generosity of God in our lives. When people see us giving, they see God's giving.

The early Christians showed the image and likeness of God in their loving relationships with each other. Generosity and giving were the primary characteristics of their little house churches. As we are transformed by faith in Jesus and gather in small communities of love, these small communities or churches should be demonstrations of the giving nature of the God we serve! Just look at the water flowing in the very first church:

> All the believers were one in heart and mind. No one claimed that any of his possessions was his own, but they shared everything they had. With great power the apostles continued to testify to the resurrection of the Lord Jesus, and much grace was upon them all. There were no needy persons among them. For from time to time those who owned lands or houses sold them, brought the money from the sales and put

it at the apostles' feet, and it was distributed to anyone as he had need. Joseph, a Levite from Cyprus, whom the apostles called Barnabas (which means Son of Encouragement), sold a field he owned and brought the money and put it at the apostles' feet. (Acts 4:32–37)

REFLECTION AND DISCUSSION

1. What did you like the most in this meditation?
2. What did you learn about yourself?
3. How will you apply this lesson to your life?
4. What did you learn about God?

The Origin of Our River

Water [was] coming out from under the threshold of the temple . . . from under the south side of the temple, south of the altar. (Ezekiel 47:1)

For God so loved the world that he gave his one and only Son, that whoever believes in him shall not perish but have eternal life. (John 3:16)

I shall never forget the first time I visited India. The pain, the suffering, and the pathos overwhelmed me. Wherever I looked it seemed dark. I rebelled.

"God, why don't you do something

about all of this?" I silently screamed in my heart.

And God said quietly, "I think I have done something."

I quieted down immediately. "Yes, God, you have. You have given your Son."

A second thought came into my mind: "What have I done? What have I given?" It was painfully obvious that I, who at that moment was judging God for not giving to India, had myself never given anything to this, the neediest of all lands.

I laughed as a third thought came to mind: When my sacrificial gift matched God's, I could come back to him with my questions. Until such a time (which would never occur) it's best that I submit to the ultimate Giver and stop accusing him of doing nothing, for all our giving is ultimately nothing more than his giving through us!

We often think of God as blissfully above our pain—someone detached from suffering. However, if you could put all of human suffering together, from Adam and Eve to this day, in one huge suffering experience—all the wars, sickness, betrayal, immorality, and cruelty—it would not begin to measure up to the pain the Savior suffered when he bore not only our punishment but all of our sin on Calvary's cross. All our pain is temporal! Christ suffered *eternal* pain, the pain of *eternal punishment* for sin when he died on the cross.

The origin of the "river of giving" lies in self-denial, and no one has denied himself more than the Father in the gift of his own Son, nor than the Son in not clinging to the rights of his position as God, but instead lowering himself by taking on our human form and even death (Philippians 2:6–11). The desire of God's heart is giving, not getting. Could there be any greater giving than God himself bearing our sins? "And the LORD has laid on him the iniquity of us all" (Isaiah 53:6b).

The river of God starts in the temple, south of the altar in Ezekiel's vision. The Old Testament altar is a symbol of the New Testament cross. The "trickle" of water flowing south of the altar symbolizes that the headwaters of God's special river of love and redemption lie in the pain and suffering of the Father and the Son at Calvary. God's giving climaxes on Calvary. The lowest spot in history, the unjust crucifixion of the only sinless human, becomes the high point of God's revelation of his generous nature. No one can imagine the suffering and the pain of that eternal hell for the Father and the Son and the Spirit at the moment when Christ cried, "My God, my God, why have you forsaken me?" (Mark 15:34b). God's generosity bears a personal price far beyond our comprehension.

A wealthy young man came to Jesus one day with a common question: "How can I be saved? What must I do to 'get' eternal life?" (see Mark 10:17). The answer Jesus gave seems perplexing and contradictory to John 3:16. Christians teach that there is nothing one can do to gain salvation. We can only accept it by faith. Jesus himself said, "Whoever believes . . . shall not perish but have eternal life." In his answer to this rich young man Jesus seems to contradict himself when he says, "Go, sell everything you have and give to the poor, and you will have treasure in heaven. Then come, follow me" (Mark 10:21).

The rich man was wealthy in two ways. He had two "piles" of possessions: He had stacks of money and stacks of good deeds. He wanted to get a third pile of wealth, namely, eternal life. He thought that eternal life was a possession we can get — a kind of eternal insurance policy. Most of us think this way. We think of heaven or salvation as a possession we can *get* through faith. If we believe certain statements and say a prayer, we can be assured that we will "get saved." But that's not so, for salvation is not a possession we can get; *it is a condition in which we are transformed to give.*

Being born again is being divinely and eternally transformed from a stagnant, dying pond to a life-giving stream. This is what Jesus was teaching this young man. He was saying, "Do you want eternal life? Let me tell you what it is. Eternal life is the condition of complete self-surrender that enables you to give your all. Heaven is eternal giving. It is not something you get, but a condition of generosity such as I and my Father demonstrated in my coming to earth to suffer and die."

Our rivers are born when we die to *getting* and start living for *giving*. Jesus defined eternal life as the death of the getting principle and the birth of the giving principle. Unfortunately many Western people think of salvation as getting another possession rather than a transformation to generosity. It was the same for the wealthy young man. He left sad, for he was devoted to the principle of getting. He had many possessions, and to inherit eternal life meant that he had to change from getting more to giving his all.

Contrast his story with that of a nine-year-old orphan girl in India who was transformed by Christ during a Mission India Children's Bible Club. Her immediate impulse was to give away what she had received. She wanted her friends to have what she had. So she asked her teacher for materials so that she could teach her friends. Her teacher said she was too young to teach, and besides they had no more workbooks. The little girl was undaunted. She said she would do it without the help of the books since she had memorized all the lessons! She rounded up her friends, all ninety of them, and held three of her own Children's Bible Clubs, teaching the Bible lessons as she remembered them. She taught each club for two weeks.

Many of her friends were transformed and started to give to their parents. And as the stream of life flowed through these little ones to their parents, within a year fifty parents had been transformed to giving and had started a little church.

That little girl understood what it means to be saved. She stopped living to get and started living to give. Immediately the "torrents" of eternal life flowed through her. The origin of the river is in conversion from getting to giving, from selfishness to sacrifice.

Salvation is not a possession to be "gotten" but a transformed condition in which we begin eternal giving.

REFLECTION AND DISCUSSION

1. Do you understand the distinction between thinking of salvation as a possession we get and a condition in which we give? Explain in your own words.
2. When does giving get costly?
3. If giving doesn't cost us anything, have we given?

The Direction of Our River

As the man went eastward with a measuring line in his hand, he measured off a thousand cubits and then led me through water that was ankle-deep. He measured off another thousand cubits and led me through water that was knee-deep. He measured off another thousand and led me through water that was up to the waist. He measured off another thousand, but now it was a river that I could not cross, because the water had risen and was deep enough to swim in—a river that no one could cross. (Ezekiel 47:3–5)

Satan's sin was reversing the direction of his "flow." Everything in heaven flows outward, like a spring of water. Even inside of God there is an "outward" flow. This is the one truth about the Trinity that we can grasp, and it must be repeated. God consists of three persons in one essence. We cannot fully understand the concept of one God who is three persons, but we can understand that the three persons of the Trinity are always flowing "out" of themselves to each other. The Father, Son, and Holy Spirit live in perfect support, love, equality, and giving to each other.

God is to be glorified, but not as one individual into whom all streams flow. Rather God is to be lifted up as the ultimate picture of outward direction, even in his very essence. One might say that God is the ultimate picture of giving relationships within himself. God is love because he exists as three persons who are constantly giving perfect love, service, and submission to each other! There is no other God like this. All other gods are individuals demanding that the "flow" be toward them and into them. The God of the Bible, the triune God, is the God of the outward flow.

Satan changed the direction of the "flow" in his heart from a river that gives, to a retaining pond. Satan wanted everything to flow into him. His is the "Kingdom of Get." God's kingdom is the "Kingdom of Give." Getting causes separation, and separation culminates in the ultimate prison of death. The inward flow separates us from society, from family, from friends, from all that is precious. The inward flow ends in death. Satan separated himself from the direction of heaven when he decided to try to "reverse the flow" in heaven and direct it into himself instead of directed out. Removed from heaven, he was separated from God's glorious giving, along with one third of the angels who also were converted from giving to getting.

C. S. Lewis captures this picture in *The Great Divorce* when he pictures hell as solitary confinement or eternal "aloneness." Napoleon walks back and forth in his cell, reciting all the wrongs done to him throughout his life, living in misery recounting all the victories denied him. His cell floats farther and farther from all living beings as he concentrates solely on the "inward direction," thinking of all the evils he endured and the possessions denied him. That's hell.

Many are bound in the hell of getting long before they die. Only at physical death do they have that hell imprison them for eternity. They live in misery, consumed with anxiety about either what they have not yet gained or what they have already lost. Fear over possessions gained or lost is the essence of hell itself. It is the "pond" mentality, which constantly measures life in the amount of "water" kept in the pond rather than the river mentality, which measures the gallons that flow and give life to all along the stream.

When God created Adam and Eve and gave them everything, including the opportunity to give love to him through obedience, Satan intercepted and reversed the course of the river. Even though Adam and Eve had been given everything, including the opportunity to love, Satan so distorted God's command and incited such longing for forbidden fruit that Adam and Eve changed from the image of God—the total outward flow of a river—into the image of Satan, a stagnant lake—always receiving but never giving. That inward direction of getting, that goal and purpose in life to accumulate for oneself, with all the consequences of separation and brokenness, has been passed down through the generations of humankind.

In John 15:1–8 Jesus gives us another word picture of the "outward" flow: the vine, the branch, and the fruit. I had a vision one cold Thanksgiving Day in which I saw myself driving through one of the many apple orchards surrounding our home. The trees were bare. Apples had been picked. Leaves had fallen. But then I noticed something very striking. In my vision I saw a strange apple tree that had kept all its apples stacked neatly in a pyramid around its trunk. Each apple was polished and beautiful and glistened in the November sunlight. I heard the apple tree praying a Thanksgiving Day prayer:

Thank you, God, that you have blessed me with so many apples. I look at all the other trees in the orchard and not one has an apple or even a leaf on its branches. I cannot understand why I am so blessed to have so many apples. Look at all the apples I have piled around my trunk. Why have you blessed me so? Thank you this Thanksgiving Day for blessing me with so much when all the other trees have so little.

And then I heard crying in heaven. It was God crying as he wept over his apple tree. He replied:

Don't you know that I did not create you to keep your apples? See all the other trees? They are not barren but have produced abundant fruit that has been given away to bless others. They are not the barren trees. You are the barren tree, for you have given nothing to others. Even now the maggots have begun to eat what is stacked around your trunk, and

soon they will penetrate your bark
and cause you, too, to die.

As I pondered the meaning of the
vision . . . I wondered how many Christians
were praising God for the apples they kept,
when they should have been praising God
for all the apples they might have given
away.

What are our thanksgiving days? Are
they celebrations of our selfishness as we
look at all we possess, or are they truly
celebrations of what we have given as we
measure our gifts and rejoice that so many
blessings have flowed out of our river?
John 15:1–8 makes it very clear: God's life
in Christ flows into us for one purpose—
to bear fruit to be given for the nourish-
ment of others.

Virtually all New Testament references
to hell are based on the failure to bear
fruit. Those who fail to give are the barren
ones. They are stagnant ponds of death
rather than flowing, life-giving rivers.
They wind up in eternal separation from
the paradise of unlimited giving.

REFLECTION AND DISCUSSION

1. What did you like best in the lesson?
2. What impressed you about God's giving?
3. Are you thankful for what you have and for what you have given?

DAY 6

The Mysterious Increase of Our River

As the man went eastward with a measuring line in his hand, he measured off a thousand cubits and then led me through water that was ankle-deep. He measured off another thousand cubits and led me through water that was knee-deep. He measured off another thousand and led me through water that was up to the waist. He measured off another thousand, but now it was a river that I could not cross, because the water had risen and was deep enough to swim in—a river that no one could cross. (Ezekiel 47:3–5)

Now to him who is able to do immeasurably more than all we ask or imagine. (Ephesians 3:20a)

53

And my God will meet all your needs according to his glorious riches in Christ Jesus. (Philippians 4:19)

A young mother was dying of cancer. She was surrounded for several months at the end of her life by a prayer team of six other mothers in her church. She shared a vision God had given her—a vision, she said, of a million souls in India streaming into heaven as a result of her witness. The prayer team thought this was a certain sign that God was going to miraculously heal her. However, shortly after seeing the vision she died.

Five years later a north Indian Christian came to the USA and located the church of this mother and her prayer team. He contacted the minister of missions and shared a little tract written by a dying mother, and inquired as to whether the minister might know anything about the author. The tract was the young mother's testimony of her love for Christ through the pain of cancer.

The young mother, who had died of cancer, had written her testimony; and that had found its way to India, been printed as a tract, and was being distributed in north India. The Indian Christian said that the tract had been widely circulated and already four new churches had been planted through it. The prayer team understood then. God's giving through us is a giving that is always expanding.

The stream begins with Christ (the hope of glory) in us, and then moves out beyond us in a continuous, constantly increasing flow. It is not dry at certain times and at flood stage at others. The river of God's generosity flows constantly and is always increasing. It does not flow in fits and spurts. There is no "dry season" in which the torrents of water are stopped up. While we may think there are dry spots in our lives and the flow from the "headwaters" of the Spirit in us may seem like a tiny trickle, we must remember that downstream, in places we cannot see, God is still at work increasing the flow of our river. Even when we are giving little, God knows; and he is still increasing what we have already given. The flow of the river that starts with our new birth always increases mysteriously, not only during our lifetime but also through the generations that follow us. We cannot see what is happening "downriver," where God is working in ways we cannot even imagine.

Much is going on "downstream" that we will know about only in glory. It is, as Paul puts it in Ephesians 3:20, a giving that brings results that are "immeasurably more than all we ask or imagine." The increasing multiplication of our giving goes on long after we leave this earth. God fulfilled his promise to the young mother for the one million souls she had seen in her vision, but did it after her translation to heaven.

This happens in the life of every believer! God always works "downstream" from every gift, where we cannot see what is going on. He will multiply the results of our giving for eternity. As Isaiah testified, "The least of you will become a thousand, the smallest a mighty nation. I am the LORD; in its time I will do this swiftly" (60:22). God has a plan for each of us. We are his living temples.

Each of us has his or her own Dead Sea into which God's Spirit flows. God is not hindered by our weakness but rather uses our weaknesses as the "holes" through which his streams of eternal life flow. Every human weakness is a new opportunity for the Spirit to pour out more of his goodness, because we, in our weakness, must rely on him; and it is our reliance on him that opens the door to let the Spirit flow through us. The more independent we are and the more we rely on our own strength, the more we shut the door to the streams of eternal life flowing through us. When Jesus said that in order to get into the kingdom of God we had to become as little children, he was teaching that being saved comes only to those who have a childlike dependency on the Father. It is this dependency that opens the continuously increasing flow.

I believe it will take an eternity to see the rivers of life that flow from each of us. Remember the little nine-year-old Indian girl who taught three Bible clubs, and how the children who came to Christ led fifty parents to become new disciples (the story we told on Day Four)? That little girl came to Christ because someone gave a dollar to Mission India. That is the total cost to allow an Indian child to come to a ten-day Bible club.

But what is God doing with that $1.00 gift right now as you read this? This little girl, brought to Christ through a tiny gift, has become the headwaters of a massive river of streams of eternal life that is continuously expanding. What is happening to those boys and girls she led to Christ? How many others are they touching? What about the families and the parents? How much living water is flowing through them?

What will it be like when we get to heaven to see the eternal consequences of every gift that we thought so inconsequential? Think of how God's giving will increase during her lifetime. Think of how it will increase throughout time until Jesus comes again in the lives of those she brought to him! Think of the surprise when the person who gave the $1.00 sees what happened through it.

Napoleon Hill, one of the leading thinkers of the "New Age" said, "What the mind can conceive, man can achieve." In lecturing on the New Age I have often pointed out that for the Christian this is one of the most limiting statements ever conceived. Why in the world would I want to limit myself to my thoughts and imaginations when I have the promise that God will do things [through my river] beyond anything I could ever dream? (See Ephesians 3:20.)

Ezekiel's guide measured the river four times. The first time it was only ankle deep. The second time it was knee deep. The third time it was waist deep. The final measurement showed that it became so deep it was impassable. Mysteriously this increase occurred without any tributaries flowing in from the outside. It was growth from within. It grew because God was the sole source, continuously increasing the flow. His resources for our giving are infinite. God's giving is continuous, unbroken, constant, and always increasing.

REFLECTION AND DISCUSSION

1. Have you seen times in your life when God has multiplied what you thought was an insignificant act of encouragement or some gift far beyond anything you dreamed possible?
2. What encouraged you the most in this meditation?
3. Give an example of a person whose impact after death far exceeded the one during his life.

The Results of Our River

Swarms of living creatures will live wherever the river flows. There will be large numbers of fish, because this water flows there and makes the salt water fresh; so where the river flows everything will live. Fishermen will stand along the shore; from En Gedi to En Eglaim there will be places for spreading nets. The fish will be of many kinds—like the fish of the Great Sea. But the swamps and marshes will not become fresh; they will be left for salt. Fruit trees of all kinds will grow on both banks of the river. Their leaves will not wither, nor will their fruit fail. Every month they will bear, because the water from the sanctuary flows to them. Their

*Fruit will serve for food and their leaves
for healing.* (Ezekiel 47:9–12)

All the old water carrier did each day
was to go back and forth from the
well to the village, delivering water. He
carried two buckets, one old and leaky and
the other new. On each trek back from the
well, so much water leaked out of the old
bucket that it was only half full. The new
one, bright and shiny, was always full.

One day the old leaky bucket said,
"Why do you continue to use me, old man?
Look at your new bucket. Each time we get
to the village it is still full, while I am half
empty. I make you work twice as hard."

The old water carrier laughed. "Ah,"
he said, "have you no idea of how you are
used each day? Haven't you seen the flowers on your side of the path? I use your
leaks to water them each time we pass
by. There are no flowers on the side of the
path where I carry the new bucket, for no
water spills on that side."

Many of us feel like that old, leaky water

bucket, and we all want to be like the new bucket, shiny and keeping our water. We don't want to be full of leaks. What does our tiny little life matter anyway? What good are we doing? We are so small and make so little impact.

But God is at work. He is flowing out of us. We may feel like a leaky water bucket. We may see few results from our efforts. But God is at work, and he will produce a harvest beyond anything we can ever imagine. There is only one way in which God gives: in abundance. God's giving through each of his children is never partial.

John wrote in his first epistle, "Behold what manner of love the Father has bestowed [lavished] on us, that we should be called children of God!" (1 John 3:1 NKJV). I love that word *behold*. I find it unfortunate that most new translations eliminate it, for it expresses surprise. "Look at this!" John shouts to us. "Look at the lavishness of God's love." The word *lavish* means to pour out in such abundance that the container overflows with it. John calls us to look at the love the Father lavishes on us. Lavishes . . . what an incredibly rich word! The Father pours out his gifts in such abundance that they overflow. His giving is like filling a glass of water so full that it overflows and spills on everything around.

Abundance is the climax of John's vision. The river brings abundant life to the Dead Sea as well as the desert around it. The Dead Sea is the most lifeless body of water on earth. Its salt content is so high that no fish can live in it, and the brine poisons all the land around it. Yet, in Ezekiel's vision, when the temple water of life flows into it, the sea is transformed so that it is swarming with fish. Wherever the water of life touches the salt water, large numbers of fish spring up. Fishermen stand along its banks with huge catches of fish. The picture is of a total transformation from barrenness to abundant life on land and in the sea.

And there were trees; amazing trees, trees that never failed to bear fruit. They bore fruit every month! Their fruit was good for food and also healing. What an awesome picture of the completeness of

God's generosity! Everywhere, everything was touched by his gifts and changed from lifelessness to abundant life.

Each time you wonder what is happening through your giving, read Ezekiel 47. Meditate on the results of the river bringing life to land and sea. God is showing you what he does "downstream" with your gifts. He perfects our giving. More than that he makes the results miraculously, supernaturally, lavishly, surprisingly beyond all we can imagine. Ezekiel's vision is our vision; it pictures what is happening each day until Christ returns.

Salvation is being changed from barrenness to productivity. Salvation is God using us as the streams of life-giving water to transform the lifeless deserts in which we live. And giving is when God produces in our lifeless deserts rich fruit-bearing gardens. God's life-giving torrents of water change our Dead Seas from lifeless waters to waters swarming with fish.

Jesus told a story about a traveler who stopped by a friend's house and asked for three loaves of bread since he had no food (Luke 11:5–8). Even though it was late at night the traveler's friend, who had no bread, went to someone who did have food and woke him up. He urgently asked for food. The first friend, although he had no bread, knew who to go to, to get bread for the hungry traveler. The "first" friend linked the hungry traveler to the second friend, who could meet his need. We are "God's links," connecting the empty people of our lives with the abundance of God. As a good friend of mine, Wilson Benton, put it, "We are friends in the middle, in the middle of the night, linking our friends to God."

We link God's resources to the needy around us by constant prayer that out of God's infinite resources their many needs might be met. God does not expect us to provide for them out of our meager resources any more than he expected that little boy to feed five thousand with a small lunch of a few pieces of bread and fish (John 6:1-14). God expects us to bring the little we have to him and let him touch it and multiply it so that it becomes plenty.

REFLECTION AND DISCUSSION

1. What did you like best in this meditation?
2. Have you ever been given a glimpse of ways God has multiplied your giving?
3. How has God used "leaks" in your own life to water the flowers in other lives?

We Give the Seven Gifts of Christ

If we spent more time reflecting on the spiritual value of what we actually are giving, our excitement about giving would dramatically increase! When we limit giving to our money or to our talents, and see what we give merely in terms of human limitations, we can easily be discouraged not to give. We downplay the importance of our gifts, whether they are gifts of money or time or service. It just doesn't matter, we think; for we look at them as if they are "our" gifts, human gifts, gifts of limited value.

Satan loves this. He wants us to think that our five loaves of bread and two fish will never feed five thousand families (John 6:1-14). He wants us to look at our gifts only in terms of human abilities and never to think of what we are really giving to others through our gifts. He wants us to feel that our giving is no more significant than a little boy throwing a single starfish back into the ocean, when there are ten thousand more stranded starfish on the beach.

Every time we give we become the channel through which the seven precious gifts of Christ flow, each a priceless gift with the greatest available power to transform. The seven gifts of Christ that flow through our gifts are his presence, his power, his provision, his perfection, his resurrection, his glorious and victorious reign, and his return to the earth to live with his people for eternity in a new world. These gifts are priceless. I may not be excited about the gift of money, or even giving comfort and counsel to someone, but when I know that Christ uses my generosity as a riverbed through which one or more of his gifts flow, then I have something that really grips me. We need to understand that every time we give, from a smile to a million dollars, we are opening the door for Christ to flow through us with one or more of these marvelous gifts!

We Give the Gift of Christ's Presence

Your attitude should be the same as that of Christ Jesus: Who, being in very nature God, did not consider equality with God something to be grasped, but made himself nothing, taking the very nature of a servant, being made in human likeness. And being found in appearance as a man, he humbled himself and became obedient to death—even death on a cross! Therefore God exalted him to the highest place and gave him the name that is above every name, that at the name of Jesus every knee should bow, in heaven and on earth and under the earth, and every tongue confess that Jesus Christ is Lord, to the glory of God the Father. (Philippians 2:5–11)

"The virgin will be with child and will give birth to a son, and they will call him Immanuel"—which means, "God with us." (Matthew 1:23)

Are you "with it"? "With it" is a phrase meaning together or in or with. When we ask someone, "Are you with us?" we are asking if they agree with us or are "with" us in our proposed task or our understanding of an argument.

What does Matthew 1:23 mean when Isaiah predicts that the Savior's name will be Immanuel (which in Hebrew is three words combined into one: *us, with,* and *God*)? Immanuel means "God with us," but what is it to have "God with us"? What does it mean to be "with it" with God? The name Immanuel is one of the most amazing names of our Savior and certainly an encouraging and enabling name. Is there anything more wonderful than to have "God with us" in every aspect of our lives?

Our eldest son, who is our pastor, illustrated the meaning of "God with us" in a very striking way in a sermon. As he was preaching, he casually walked down from the pulpit and out into the crowded, four-hundred-seat auditorium, where he stopped about halfway up the middle aisle and shook hands with "Frank." He asked Frank how he was and if he was enjoying the sermon and having a good day. He then continued preaching as he walked further and stopped and shook hands with a teen-ager and interrupted himself as he started to converse with the young person. Then while resuming preaching, he climbed up to the balcony and interrupted himself again by conversing with someone there. Coming down from the balcony he actu-ally left the auditorium and went into the nursery to talk to some of the little ones before coming back to the pulpit.

It was his way of illustrating the difference between talking to someone or talking with someone, the difference between communication and conversa-tion. Communication, or the sharing of ideas, can exist without conversation. Communication is a one-way street; some-one preaches or teaches and the rest listen.

Conversation is a two-way relationship in which we share mutually. Good conversation includes communication or the explanation of a concept. But it is much more.

Conversation is communion. We bind ourselves together by listening and sharing. Talking *to* someone is a legitimate activity. It is the primary method by which God related to Israel in the Old Testament. However, talking *with* someone is far more personal and intimate. Talking *with* each other (not *to* each other) involves listening and reacting. It involves agreement and bonding together. It involves bringing hope and help to each other. It involves much more than mere communication. It results in bonding, friendship, love, and mutual concern. In talking with each other we reach the high point of friendship.

When Jesus came, our relationship with God changed from God talking to us, to God talking with us. Our relationship changed from communication to conversation, from being his servants to being his friends. "I no longer call you servants, because a servant does not know his master's business. Instead, I have called you friends, for everything that I learned from my Father I have made known to you" (John 15:15).

The concept of God *with us* is the most referred to doctrine about God in the New Testament. Our relationship with Christ is described 174 times in the New Testament as being "in" Christ. Being "in" Christ is something like the phrase with which we started: "with it." To be "with it" means to be "in" the group, to be "in" on the idea or the project. To be in Christ means to be with Christ in every moment of your life. Christ himself describes being with him even more powerfully when he talks about our relationship as that of a branch to the vine (John 15:1–8).

Sometimes at night I look into the cloudless sky and wonder about those twinkling little diamonds. Who is this God who created it all and gives energy to keep it all spinning and expanding? I think of billions and billions of stars in our own galaxy and billions upon billions of galaxies. How can it be that a God without dimensions could limit himself to the dimension of a human form and be called Immanuel, "God with us"?

Who can comprehend the promises of Revelation 21?

> Now the dwelling of God is with men, and he will live with them. They will be his people, and God himself will be with them and be their God. He will wipe every tear from their eyes. There will be no more death or mourning or crying or pain, for the old order of things has passed away. (vv. 3–4)

When we give as believers, we are giving this presence of Christ to others. It is the greatest gift that can be given. It is the gift of the Creator of the universe becoming our intimate friend. He doesn't talk *to* us but rather talks *with* us, as a friend does with a friend. Is there a gift greater than ending the separation between us and God? I know of none. Is there a privilege greater than to be entrusted with this, the greatest of all gifts — the gift of his friendship and presence?

Our giving starts with the gift of Christ's presence. We are to bring Christ to every village, every people group, every slum, every city, every workplace, every school, and every apartment complex— we are to bring Christ to every human being. We are to do this through calling Christians of all groups to work together, systematically saturating neighborhoods with prayer cells in which people are taught how to "converse" with God, not just "talk to" God.

Neighborhoods in all parts of the world, including the great cities of America, have been dramatically changed when Christians gave the presence of Christ to the area through forming neighborhood prayer cells. Prayer is conversation with God as we speak with him, and listen to him reply to us.

REFLECTION AND DISCUSSION

1. What did you like best in this meditation?
2. What are some of the ways in which God speaks with us?
3. How can you tell if it is God who is speaking?

4. Are you a member of a prayer cell in which people are hearing God speak to them through each other?

We Give the Power of Christ

But you will receive power when the Holy Spirit comes on you; and you will be my witnesses in Jerusalem, and in all Judea and Samaria, and to the ends of the earth. (Acts 1:8)

While attending a Children's Bible Club in India a young boy found Jesus. And he knew that Jesus had power far greater than the local witchdoctor's power. That witchdoctor had cursed his grandmother years ago with the curse of thorns. Every Thursday and Saturday ("devil days" in the village), she could not walk because of the thorn-like pain in her joints, which would come like clockwork. This crippling pain was a continual testimony to the witchdoctor's supernatural power.

The little boy hurried to his grandmother's home that day when he first heard about the power of Jesus and saw that power in the Children's Bible Club prayer group. Amazing things were happening when the boys and girls were praying to Jesus.

Her home was a little hut with a low door, which forced her to stoop as she entered. All "untouchables" (as grandma was) had to have low doors, making them stoop down upon entering their homes. It was a reminder of their low position in the village.

He told his grandma he had found a God more powerful than the witchdoctor. Grandma refused to believe. She reminded her grandson that over the past twenty years, she had sacrificed countless chickens and goats to appease the witchdoctor, pleading for the removal of the curse and the relief of her pain. But her disbelief did not deter her grandson. He prayed for healing in the name of Jesus.

Grandma felt fire go through all her joints. Slowly, gently she stood up, gingerly taking a few steps to the little door. She stooped down and walked through the door and out of her little hut. And then she danced down the dusty street! The villagers were amazed. "What God has done this?" they asked. "Who is more powerful than the witch doctor?" Old Grandma said she did not know who this God was who healed her, but her grandson did.

"His name is Jesus," the little boy said. "When we pray in the name of Jesus his power flows, and that power cured my grandma! His name is powerful, more powerful than all the demons!" And the entire village, looking at Grandma, wanted to know more. The grandson shared the little he knew from the Children's Bible Club lessons, and most of the villagers believed.

This little boy understood that Jesus had transformed him. Although no one had ever told him, he understood that he was a "royal priest" (1 Peter 2:9 NLT), and in Jesus' name he had more power than the witchdoctor. Jesus had given him his name to use. Using the name of Jesus, he experienced power exceeding the power of any of the witchdoctors, the priests of demons. The name of Jesus is the power to cast out any demon and to work miracle upon miracle.

Jesus promises us that where two or three are gathered in prayer, Christ will be there with all of his power (Matthew 18:19–20). Through this little cluster of boys and girls in a Children's Bible Club, a boy became the doorway for Christ's power, which flowed through his prayer and cured his grandmother.

When small prayer cells form in villages in India, or in neighborhoods in the West, Jesus moves into the neighborhood, and the supernatural power of Jesus transforms the village, just as it did for that little boy and his grandmother. Whenever we bring the presence of Jesus to a village or area by forming a House of Prayer (a prayer cell), we bring the personal power of Jesus.

The power of Jesus' name is rooted in the fact that when Christ died on Calvary he "disarmed the powers and authorities" and "made a public spectacle of them, triumphing over them by the cross" (Colossians 2:15). And at that same name, Paul likewise writes in Philippians, every knee will bow someday and every tongue confess that Jesus Christ is Lord (2:10–11).

Western Christians don't realize that each of our neighborhoods, like every village in the world, is a spiritual prison; and we wrestle first of all, not with human beings, but with principalities and powers, with spiritual forces of evil in the heavenly realms. Christ gave us binding power through unified prayer, promising that what we bind on earth he will bind in the heavenly places (Matthew 18:18).

Our lack of transforming power is a direct result of our lack of prayer. Our failure to bring transformation comes through our lack of prayer to bind the spiritual forces of evil with Christ's power at our disposal. With that powerful name we can move across the nations reclaiming villages and cities, neighborhoods and districts from demonic powers for Jesus. Christ has given us power over demons. He tells us that at his name, the demons will flee. This was the experience of the first disciples when they were sent out two by two into the villages: "Lord, even the demons submit to us in your name" (Luke 10:17).

Peter tells us that we are "royal priests" (1 Peter 2:9 NLT). The word *royal* means ruling. We are ruling priests. God is training us to be his ruling priests, a position we will hold in the new earth for all eternity. God created us to rule the world. The devil temporarily wrested dominion over all the earth from us. Jesus has defeated the devil through his death on the cross and has reclaimed authority over the world for all his followers (Colossians 2:15). We are now in the process of reclaiming that authority.

The second gift we have to give is the gift of his powerful name! As we speak his name, demonic powers tremble, flee, and fall away. Miracles will be performed. People will be set free (Luke 4:18). When we give of ourselves we are opening the windows of heaven to allow the binding power of Christ over evil to flow out and transform the entire landscape. Deserts will blossom like rose gardens when God's people pray for transformation!

REFLECTION AND DISCUSSION

1. What did you like in this lesson?
2. Have you had experiences of powerful answers to prayer in Jesus' name? Share them.
3. Are we more reluctant to recognize demonic power than people in India and Africa? If so, why?

We Give Christ's Provisions

Ask and it will be given to you; seek and you will find; knock and the door will be opened to you. For everyone who asks receives; he who seeks finds; and to him who knocks, the door will be opened. Which of you, if his son asks for bread, will give him a stone? Or if he asks for a fish, will give him a snake? If you, then, though you are evil, know how to give good gifts to your children, how much more will your Father in heaven give good gifts to those who ask him! (Matthew 7:7–11)

The old song says, "Count your many blessings, name them one by one, / And it will surprise you what the Lord has done." As we move through the life of Christ, we are naming his gifts, given to us to share with others. We are examining the gifts he has given us, not for ourselves only, but to be shared with everyone, everywhere.

How has Christ provided for us? What wealth has he entrusted to us, not only for our good but also to share with everyone, everywhere? Christ teaches us the nature of his provision in the great "I am" statements found in the gospel of John. These cover all the needs of any human being; and as Christ's friends—his royal priests—we are appointed to share these gifts with the world.

I Am the Good Shepherd (John 10:11, 14)

Christ provides for us as a shepherd provides for his sheep. A shepherd knows his sheep, and Christ knows us. He knows our days, our minutes. He has a plan for us, a good plan, not an evil one. "'For I know the plans I have for you,' declares the LORD, 'plans to prosper you and not to harm you, plans to give you hope and a future'" (Jeremiah 29:11).

A shepherd *plans* every move for his sheep. A shepherd *protects* his sheep from all danger. He keeps them from harm. He wants the sheep to *prosper*. No provision could be made that is greater than the provision of having Jesus Christ as the Good Shepherd, who plans, protects, and provides for us in every way. To trust him means perfect peace, peace beyond the paltry power of positive thinking.

Jesus is the Good Shepherd and is so dedicated that he died so that we might be protected. How can we fear or doubt the future when he has done so much for us? And how can we keep to ourselves the gift of the Good Shepherd's planning for each life, protecting each one for eternity, and providing all we need? How can we neglect to share it with others?

I Am the Gate . . . I Am the Way
(John 10:9; 14:6)

Jesus is the only door and the only way to salvation. This exclusive claim sets

Christians apart and often irritates others who claim that the followers of Christ are arrogant and proud. The fact remains, however, that of all religious leaders and gurus, only Jesus is alive. No other founder of a religion or guru of the past has risen from the dead, and since they are all dead, they are all unable to be the path to eternal life.

Christianity is not a religion. Rather it is a love relationship with a living Savior who died and rose again. What a wonder of wonders that we have been provided a different pathway of salvation, one that comes not by keeping the law but by faith in the righteousness of the living Jesus Christ (Romans 3:21–22). Jesus has come to set captives free: "You will know the truth, and the truth will set you free" (John 8:32). The provision of a way out of the eternal prison of sin and hell is without doubt the most priceless gift. We have received this gift to share with others.

I Am the Bread of Life (John 6:35)
Only Christ can satisfy fully and eternally. He is the spiritual bread that makes us full

forever. He is the water of life that quenches the empty, driving thirst within us. How many millions wander from one god to another, from one religion to another, from spiritual quests to total atheism, because they are so empty? Do we have a passion to give this provision to others?

I Am the Light of the World (John 9:5)
Spiritual darkness is so fearful that it drives multitudes to suicide. Is there anything more frightening than long-ing for the truth and being unable to find it? Jesus claims that he is the Light, he is the Truth, he can show us the wonder of God. What an utterly amazing thought that the Creator became the crea-ture—God-man—in order to bring light. In Jesus we can see the nature of God, the wonder of his goodness, generosity, and love. Isaiah tells us that "darkness covers the earth, and thick darkness is over the peoples" (Isaiah 60:2). Darkness creates fear. It causes stumbling and pain.

We have the light. As Christ the Light of the world dwells in us we begin to "glow." Our giving "turns on the lights." As we glow with Christ's presence we provide Christ's light for others to find their way in the darkness.

I Am the Vine (John 15:1)

Jesus provides life for us just as the vine provides life for its branches. So intimate is our relationship with this living Lord that we share in his life. It is that life, that indwelling Spirit, which produces fruit that lasts for eternity. Jesus provides us protection, rescue, satisfaction, light to know, and life to live. He entrusts these provisions to us to share with others!

What do we have to give? We have the gifts of Christ to give! We don't give throwaway gifts. We give gifts that last for eternity when we give the gift of Christ to the world. How can a Christian be selfish? How can a Christian keep Christ's provisions to himself and deny the world the knowledge that all they need is in Jesus? We are called to share Christ's presence, power, and provision with everyone, everywhere.

REFLECTION AND DISCUSSION

1. Which of the five "I am" statements is most important to you?
2. How does this meditation motivate you to share Christ's provision?
3. Name one practical way you can share these gifts with someone this week.

We Give the Gift of Christ's Perfection

But now God has shown us a different way to heaven — not by "being good enough" and trying to keep his laws, but by a new way (though not new, really, for the Scriptures told about it long ago). Now God says he will accept and acquit us—declare us "not guilty"—if we trust Jesus Christ to take away our sins. (Romans 3:21–22 TLB)

I magine," our son said in a sermon. "Imagine that you are a pregnant wife and are sitting at the breakfast table. Your husband, sitting across from you, faces you. You dare not look him in the eye. He knows. You know. The child within your womb is not his. You have been unfaithful. You dare not lift your head.

"And then quietly, gently, he reaches across the table and takes your chin in his hand. Lifting your face he forces you to look at him. 'I know,' he quietly says. 'I forgive. I will forgive. It will be as if it never happened. You are, and will always be, my wife! And I shall accept the child as my own.'"

Can someone do that? Perhaps they can, but such unconditional love is rare. One thing is certain—we cannot cleanse each other of our sin. Only God can do that. Only God can clothe us with the righteous robes of Jesus Christ. He alone can cover us with his Son's perfection!

That is the fourth gift of the life of Christ that we are entrusted to give to the world. It is the gift of *perfection*. God the Father gives to us the perfect life of Christ as our own life. He "clothes" us in the righteous robes of the Savior. He looks at us and sees only the perfection of his own Son. And then he commissions us to share that gift with others.

I have studied India for over thirty-five years, and it seems to me that there is no nation that works harder to please angry gods. Every meal and every bath, every planting and every harvest, every conversation and contact with others—all of life is done in fear of angering the gods.

I recall how one Indian woman wept as she shared her misery with us. "Do you know what it means to be a Brahmin?" she asked. "Do you know the daily fear I have lived with all my life? How could I escape offending the gods? Every part of my life was related to them. Every day—every moment it seemed—I was frightened that in some way, through some neglect or some twisting of a ritual, I would incur their wrath. My whole life was sacrificed to them.

"And then I met him, the true God, Jesus Christ! And suddenly I knew that he had forgiven all my sins. He washed me and clothed me with his perfection. I was whiter than snow. I now had a God who supplied my perfection for me. I could not make myself acceptable to him; but *he* made me acceptable!"

Tears of joy and relief flowed down her face as she spoke of the discovery of Jesus and the perfect righteousness he imparted to her through faith. She knew that, in God's sight, she would forever be acceptable to him as his perfect daughter because she was covered with the perfection of the Savior!

When God forgives he does more than forgive. He obliterates our sin. He wipes it out. Remember the husband talking to his unfaithful wife, saying, "I forgive"? He does not have the power to make her clean. Only God does. Listen to what God says: "'Come now, let us reason together,' says the LORD. 'Though your sins are like scarlet, they shall be as white as snow; though they are red as crimson, they shall be like wool'" (Isaiah 1:18).

And we all can be saved in this same way, by coming to Christ, no matter who we are or what we have been like. Yes, all have sinned; all fall short of God's glorious ideal; yet now God declares us "not guilty" of offending him if we trust in Jesus

Christ, who in his kindness freely takes away our sins. (Romans 3:23–24 TLB)

In saving us Christ did two things. First, he lived a perfect life as our substitute. Second, he died and bore eternal hell as punishment for our sin. It is not enough to have our sins paid for and then to remain in our sins. God declares that only the sinless enter his kingdom, and we need perfection. We cannot manufacture or attain it. In love, the Father covers each of us with the perfect life of Christ. He clothes us in the robes of righteousness.

When water is put in a vessel, the water goes where the pot is placed. So when we are in Christ, we are where Christ is spiritually. Being in Christ means that we are in his perfection! He perfectly obeyed the law. In Matthew 5:17 Christ says, "Do not think that I have come to abolish the Law or the Prophets; I have not come to abolish them but to fulfill them." Christ fulfilled the entire law for us. Starting with the attitudes of his heart and his most inward thoughts, to every external deed, Christ was absolutely sinless. And since we are "in" Christ, that perfection is given to us as our very own.

The illustration we began with breaks down at this point, for the husband can only forgive his wife; he cannot restore her to perfection. But God can do it for us! What a gift: to know that in God's sight I am only through the perfection of Christ. It is as if I had never sinned.

This is the fourth gift we have to give. How can we keep it from others? If we understand it and treasure it, we will be driven to share it! Often we think our gifts are merely money or time or consideration of others—we see them only in terms of human gifts.

REFLECTION AND DISCUSSION

1. What did you like best in this meditation?
2. What feelings do you have when you realize that you are "clothed" with Christ's perfection and when God looks at you he sees only the sinless life of his Son?

3. How would your life be different if you had to please angry gods instead of having Christ's gift of perfection?

We Give the Gift of Christ's Resurrection

And if Christ has not been raised, our preaching is useless and so is your faith. . . . When you sow, you do not plant the body that will be, but just a seed. . . . So will it be with the resurrection of the dead. The body that is sown is perishable, it is raised imperishable.
(1 Corinthians 15:14, 37, 42)

I remember it so well. It happened in my second church when I was still a very young, inexperienced pastor. A beautiful five-year-old girl, on her first day going to school, ran out in front of the school bus; and a car, racing by, hit her and killed her instantly.

She was the youngest of four children. The two brothers and her older sister and her mom and dad were paralyzed with grief. She was their precious little girl. The family revolved around her. Suddenly she was gone. I tried as best I could to comfort them, but I was so full of grief myself that I am afraid I was not much help. I did manage to get through reading Scripture and praying with them; and later at the funeral service, I somehow managed not to break down. I even completed the graveside services. But then I lost it as we turned to leave the cemetery. I wept.

Her brother watched us. He had made his peace with his sister's departure; and now he was very curious about all the crying, especially after all those wonderful words of comfort, and perhaps most of all when he saw me weeping. He turned to his mom and said, "Mom, why is everyone crying? Isn't Susan really in heaven with Jesus after all?"

It was one of those moments when God spoke clearly and powerfully. Even now, over forty years later, I can still hear that little boy's words as if it were only an hour ago. Oh, for the faith of a child.

I think of a little Indian boy just before he died. He had accepted Christ as his Savior and two days later said to the Children's Bible Club teacher that he was not feeling well. The teacher, noticing that something was seriously wrong, took him to a doctor. Upon examining him, they immediately placed him in the hospital. His parents were called, and the teacher and parents stood around that hospital bed later that evening. The doctor told them, in the boy's presence, that he probably would die by midnight. He had been bitten by a rabid dog, and the disease had spread beyond any cure.

The little boy, hearing the death verdict, smiled — he *smiled*!

"Mommy, Daddy, don't be alarmed," he said. "I am going to go home to my mansion tonight. I learned that Jesus is preparing a mansion in heaven for all those who believe in him. I gave my heart to him two days ago, and now he wants me with him already. Please don't cry. When I go, I won't need my clothes anymore, so give them to the children in my Bible Club." And then, turning to his teacher, he added, "Help my mommy and daddy to understand that I will be with Jesus. Bring them to Jesus too." By midnight the Savior had called him home.

The hope and belief of the Christian in the resurrection of Christ from the dead is one of the most glorious and comforting gifts of Christ entrusted to our care to give to everyone. And just think—it cost Mission India only a dollar to share the gift of Christ's resurrection with a little boy in India two days before he died—a little boy secure in the knowledge that because Christ arose and lives, he too would live after his physical death.

I'll never forget hearing the tragic news in 1999 about missionary Graham Staines. I can imagine the scene so vividly. The terrorists gathered around the jeep at midnight. Quietly they laid the straw under it and poured gas on the straw. They did not want to awaken the sleeping missionary and his two sons who were spending the night in their vehicle in a remote Indian village. They pushed long poles against the doors to prevent the three from escaping and then tossed lighted matches on the gas. They watched with glee as the gas exploded, lighting the straw, and then the flames engulfed the jeep. Graham Staines and his two sons struggled to get out but they kept them pinned in the jeep with the three poles and watched as the three were burned to death.

As the gruesome deed was reported throughout the news media in India and around the world, people mourned nationwide. *India Today*, one of the leading national news magazines, published a cross on its cover with a map of India nailed to it. A missionary and his two sons had been burned to death. How could India have fallen to such depths? Three days later, at the funeral of her husband and two sons, Mrs. Staines and her daughter sang a gospel song, which was broadcast across India.

God sent His Son; they called Him Jesus. / He came to love, heal, and forgive / He lived and died to buy my pardon; / An empty grave is there to prove my Savior lives. / Because He lives, I can face tomorrow / Because He lives, all fear is gone; / Because I know He holds the future, / And life is worth the living just because He lives.

God's Word promises there will be a resurrection of all believers because Jesus lives. "The body that is sown is perishable, it is raised imperishable; it is sown in dishonor, it is raised in glory; it is sown in weakness, it is raised in power; it is sown a natural body, it is raised a spiritual body" (1 Corinthians 15:42–44).

Think of it! God imparts to us a perfection that enables us to experience eternal life. With that perfection he gives us the assurance that not only will we have eternal life, but our bodies will be raised from the grave never again subject to pain, sickness, and death.

No farmer goes into the field in the spring, sowing seed and crying. Spring is the time of anticipation, the anticipation felt by the little Indian boy who excitedly told his parents not to cry for he was going to his "mansion." Giving is far more than giving money. In reality we don't have anything since we are merely stewards of God's treasures. The funds he entrusts to us are to be used to create channels through which the great gifts of Christ flow out to the world, including the gift of his resurrection through which we are given eternal life.

REFLECTION AND DISCUSSION

1. What did you like best in this meditation?
2. Why is the resurrection more comforting than reincarnation?
3. Mahatma Gandhi once said that if Christians are persecuted they will grow like weeds, but if left alone they will die. What is your reaction to his statement?

We Give the Comfort of Christ's Eternal Reign

And we know that in all things God works for the good of those who love him, who have been called according to his purpose. . . . What, then, shall we say in response to this? If God is for us, who can be against us? He who did not spare his own Son, but gave him up for us all—how will he not also, along with him, graciously give us all things? (Romans 8:28, 31–32)

It seems that the world is falling apart. Financial markets are a mess. Greed and corruption rule. Crime increases. Politicians are arrested and imprisoned. Terrorism abounds. As I write, I think of the outbreak of terrorism in the world's largest democracy, India. It is planned and deliberate. It is not just the burning of two five-star hotels in Mumbai, but the far more brutal rape and murder of the Christians in several regions in the state of Orissa in 2008.

The police and the state government stood idly by while Christians were raped, burned, and beheaded. Entire villages were destroyed. The atrocities were unimaginable. In the light of all this horror, I can't help but think of a seemingly ironic poem by Elizabeth Browning that my father kept on his bedroom wall, which was printed under a lovely scene of nature and ended with the words, "God's in his heaven, and all's right with his world."

It certainly doesn't seem that way, does it. Is Jesus really reigning? And what difference does it make? What comfort and courage is there in the fact that Jesus is at the right hand of God, reigning over all events of history? (See Ephesians 1:19–22.) Does he concern himself with your personal life? Is the reign of Christ something that we should announce to the world as a gift? How can we believe in such a reign when there is so much grief, corruption, evil, and cruelty?

Paul tells us that all things work together for good for those who love God (Romans 8:28ff.). We are assured that because Christ rules he will either avert all evil from our lives, or turn it out for good.

Paul also gives us many glorious reasons why our Savior's reign in heaven is of such profound comfort as we face persecution and the evils of this life. Romans 8:1 says that there is no condemnation to those who are in Christ Jesus. I am free from the punishment I justly deserve for my sins; not only free but I am covered by the perfect righteousness of Jesus Christ. I know that this is complete. The victory is finished and won, for my Savior has risen and now reigns and rules. His work is complete.

My present suffering is not worth comparing to the weight of future glory (Romans 8:18). The victory of Christ is so all encompassing, his rule and authority are so total and complete, that the suffering we go through now is only like a feather weight compared to the wonder of the glory that is yet to come. Because Christ reigns, he will work in all the evil in the lives of those who love him so that it will be turned out for good (Romans 8:28). No matter how hard the circumstances, how evil the day, Christ promises that he will protect us and use the evil for good. He will never be defeated.

Since Jesus now reigns in glory and all is beneath his power and authority, who can defeat us? (See Romans 8:31.) We are engaged in the final operations of the war; the victory over Satan is assured since Christ is reigning at the right hand of the heavenly Father. We can go now, as appointed ambassadors, into the world in the name of the King of Kings and claim it for our Savior.

Because Christ reigns, no one can ever separate us from the love of God (Romans 8:39). He has defeated all his enemies. No one is left to challenge him. Thus we know that nothing, no one, no event, no power, no angel, and no authority can ever come between us and God again.

This is the confidence that comforted an Indian pastor during the persecution in Orissa in 2008 when he returned from hiding in the jungle with his family for several days to his burned-out church and wrecked home. He was surrounded by his moderate Hindu and Muslim neighbors, who upon seeing his gracious and loving demeanor, asked him who is this Jesus who could make a man so forgiving. The pastor wrote us that in the following two weeks they baptized more new followers of Christ than the combined total of baptisms in the previous seven years.

I also think of Gloria, our precious neighbor, who endured six weeks of excruciating pain before she died. She was unable to lie down in bed and had to sit up during those pain-filled days at the end of her life. Anyone with any sympathy would say, "Why, God?" I certainly did, and in trying to comfort her three days before she died, I said, "Soon, Gloria, all your questions will be answered." Through her pain she softly replied that I was completely wrong. "No, John," she whispered. "All my questions will be irrelevant in the wonder of his glory and beauty."

No, we don't have an answer for the persecution in Orissa, for the hate-filled violence and destruction. We can say it's demonic, but that is little comfort. But we can join in Gloria's hope that when we see him, our Savior, all our questions will suddenly be irrelevant in the awesome sight of his beauty and love.

Jesus reigns. He works in ways that are far beyond comprehension, but this we know, and this assurance we give to others: Christ reigns from heaven above. And because he lives and reigns, we know that all will be right. He has entrusted this unfathomable comfort to us to share with the world through our giving.

REFLECTION AND DISCUSSION

1. What did you like best in this meditation?
2. What impact should Christ's reign have on our willingness to witness?
3. What difference does the victory of Christ have on our facing persecution and suffering?

We Give the Comfort of Christ's Return

Then I saw a new heaven and a new earth, for the first heaven and the first earth had passed away, and there was no longer any sea. I saw the Holy City, the new Jerusalem, coming down out of heaven from God, prepared as a bride beautifully dressed for her husband. And I heard a loud voice from the throne saying, "Now the dwelling of God is with men, and he will live with them. They will be his people, and God himself will be with them and be their God. He will wipe every tear from their eyes. There will be no more death or mourning or crying or pain, for the old order of things has passed away." (Revelation 21:1–4)

The sea is the Bible's symbol of separation. John was separated and imprisoned by the sea, and so it was that he wrote in Revelation 21:1 that in heaven there would "be no more sea." There are multitudes of things that separate us as humans: language, culture, race, residence, work, incomes, hatred, fighting, pride, war, crime, and prison. But only one form of separation is irreversible: death. Other forms of separation can be reversed, even if they often are not. But death cannot be reversed—not by natural means, anyway. Few have seen people come back to "life" here on this earth, and if they have, their second life is only temporary. This world is not our permanent home.

We cling to the hope of a new life, a life in heaven. And for most people that heaven is "up there" somewhere. Revelation 21:1–4 predicts the opposite, however. We won't go "up" to heaven to be with God, but surprisingly God will come down to live with us on a new earth. "I saw the Holy City, the new Jerusalem, coming *down*, out of heaven" (Revelation 21:2, emphasis added). We don't go "up" to live in this new society called "The Holy City, the new Jerusalem"; it comes *down* to exist without end on a new earth. "And I heard a loud voice from the throne saying, 'Now the dwelling of God is with men, and he will live with them. They will be his people, and God himself will be with them and be their God" (Revelation 21:3).

This earth of course will not be the same. The Bible tells us that it will be purged and the "old order of things" will pass away (Revelation 21:4). The sea will be no more; it will be an existence without any more separation. That old order of things will disappear. All mourning, sorrow, sickness, death, and separation will be gone. We will be united in a glorious, never-ending new society from which all evil has been expelled. The sun and moon will not be needed any longer, for Christ's glory will fill the earth with unending light. There will be no night.

John sees it as a vision of an eternal wedding of a beautiful bride and her husband. A vast multitude, which John says cannot be counted, drawn from every tribe, language, people, and nation will come down from their temporary home to dwell on a new earth (Revelation 7:9). Christ will receive them as his "bride," and there will be an eternal love relationship that is beyond description. This new society will be an eternally growing society.

My father used to tell me that all his hopes in heaven will not be fulfilled. He would then cite three things that he would find in heaven that could never be sated, as he repeated 1 Corinthians 13:13 (NKJV): "And now abide faith, hope, love." We will still need faith, for we will never understand everything about God. We will trust God and each other perfectly, for it will be a perfect society. We will still always be hoping in the sense that we will be eternally anticipating new discoveries about a limitless God and his boundless love. We will always be filled with excitement and anticipation at our next discovery. Heaven can never be static—a place of eternally sitting around, which I used to dread as a boy.

But the greatest of all will be the perfect love—the perfect, unmarred eternal giving that will characterize our lives for all eternity! The joyous discovery of new dimensions of giving in God will be unlimited, for God is infinite and without any limits!

And when he returns, all will see him, for he will descend on the clouds of heaven in the same way he left. This was the promise of the angels to the disciples as they stood peering into the sky. "'Men of Galilee,' they said, 'why do you stand here looking into the sky? This same Jesus, who has been taken from you into heaven, will come back in the same way you have seen him go into heaven'" (Acts 1:11).

The creation will be made new. The death principle will be removed from it, and Paul tells us that all creation groans as it awaits this glorious moment (Romans 8:19). The earth will be purified, burned by fire, and God will remake it as the home of the Savior. We will not need the sun for warmth or light, for Christ will be in our midst. We can only dream of heaven, but even in our wildest imaginations we cannot envision what glory and wonder will mark this new life. This eternal paradise with Christ is the ultimate gift that we give.

Summary: The Seven Gifts of Christ

When we think of giving, we must remember what we give! These seven presents are the ultimate gifts that we can give to others. What are the results of giving Christ's presence, provision, power, and perfection to others? What does it mean to give Christ's resurrection from the dead and the assurance that all has meaning because of Christ's reign? What hope do we give when we know that the earth will be remade and Christ will dwell here with a multitude no one can number, drawn from all the nations (Revelation 7:9)? Each time we witness, each time we comfort, each time we financially enable the good news to be spread, we are ultimately giving these seven gifts of Christ.

It is not merely money that we give. Money is only the riverbed through which these seven awesome gifts of Christ flow. Jesus told us in John 7:38–39 that the Spirit of God himself would flow from us in torrents of living water. We would become "river heads" and "wellsprings" as the seven life-giving gifts of the Savior flow through us. Our love, our care for the poor, our visiting the sick, our caring for the sorrowing—all are the riverbeds of these seven indescribable gifts of Christ. He gives these gifts only through our giving to others. Just think of what that statement means for you, for your giving. As ones commissioned to deliver the seven gifts of Christ, the followers of Jesus are the most important persons in the world. As one in whom Christ dwells, you are the channel through whom these seven indescribable gifts flow.

REFLECTION AND DISCUSSION

1. What did you like in this meditation?
2. Are you excited about Christ's return? Why or why not?
3. Summarize the seven gifts of Christ that have been entrusted to you.

Our Giving Is God's Opportunity to Give

". . . Test me in this," says the LORD Almighty, "and see if I will not throw open the floodgates of heaven and pour out so much blessing that you will not have room enough for it." (Malachi 3:10)

We often fail to see the vertical dimension in our giving. When we give we become a means by which God gives! We are his faucets! He has appointed us as his ambassadors and he will not "go around us." Our giving opens the floodgates of heaven, according to Malachi 3:10, actually affecting the way God gives. We are the "riverbeds" through which his giving flows, and failure to give resists his giving.

Let's consider this another way: Our giving is the key that opens the windows of heaven and allows the rain of God's abundance to fall. In fact, God also uses the opportunity of our gift to multiply that gift beyond all we ask or imagine (Ephesians 3:20).

This week we answer the question of "what does God do when we give?" So often when we make a gift we fail to see the way God acts in response to our giving. We do not see beyond the human gift. This "short-sighted" view of giving keeps us from giving generously and from seeing the miracles that God does in response to our giving.

We will examine seven stories of giving: four from the Old Testament and three from the New Testament. Our purpose is to discover in each the way in which God gave *after the initial human gift was made.* Our giving is only the key, the catalyst, the opportunity for God to begin his giving through us. The stream of God's life will not flow from within us until we start giving. Our generosity releases God's stream of infinite life, love, and miracles, which will continue long after we have forgotten the gift.

Each story centers on an overwhelming need compared to a pitifully small human gift; the gift seems completely out of proportion to the need. But when the little, weak human gift is given freely, generously, and in love, God joins us in giving exceedingly, abundantly above all we ask or imagine.

> Now to him who is able to do immeasurably more than all we ask or imagine, according to his power that is at work within us, to him be glory in the church and in Christ Jesus throughout all generations, for ever and ever! Amen. (Ephesians 3:20–21).

> And my God shall supply all your need according to His riches in glory by Christ Jesus. (Philippians 4:19 NKJV)

The Widow's Gift Gave God the Opportunity To Multiply

Elijah said to [the widow], "Don't be afraid. Go home and do as you have said. . . . She went away and did as Elijah had told her. So there was food every day for Elijah and for the woman and her family. (1 Kings 17:13, 15)

Elijah was on the run from King Ahab after having delivered God's message of drought and famine to that evil king. God prepared a comfortable place for

Elijah to hide along the brook in the Kerith Ravine. With ample water and bread supplied by ravens, he was well cared for in this hiding place.

However, the brook dried up and the birds left and the bread disappeared, and Elijah became a victim of the famine he had predicted. He had to move.

He went to a "foreign" land, a land the Jews believed to be filled with untouchable people. There he found a poverty-stricken widow on the verge of starvation. It is here that we face one of the most remarkable stories of how the gift of a starving widow's last meal opened the floodgates of heaven and enabled God to multiply her gift for years.

Elijah's Need

Compared to his need for the coming year, her resources were laughable. Elijah needed water, food, and a hiding place. His life was threatened by both the drought and by the hatred of the king. His previous hiding place had mysteriously dried up. No more food or water was available; hence he had to move on. God had provided miraculously. Why did the miracles stop? Why had God failed now to provide for his servant?

Many Indian evangelists, church planters, and missionaries face questions like this. Why, when they are willing to risk their lives, are they in such constant danger? Like Elijah, they don't know where their next meal is coming from. Their lives are not comfortable, pleasant, or prosperous. They are always running and hiding.

God uses these circumstances to teach us to trust in him. When one lesson is done we move to another, which often means when one trial is over another comes. God leads us into strange places to show the supernatural care he has for his own.

Her Lack

Elijah met a poor widow here, a starving woman down to her last meal. She had a precious son at home and was gathering a handful of firewood so that she could go home, make her last meal, and die! Elijah asked her for a drink. That she could handle, for there was water. She agreed to get the prophet a drink of water.

But then Elijah asked for something more, something beyond her resources; he asked a starving, poor, untouchable widow for food. She had no food to speak of, only the little bit that was left for the last meal she planned to serve her son. Surely the prophet could not expect to take the last bit of food out of a poor widow's mouth. And yet that was precisely what Elijah asked for, but he asked in the light of God's promise: "The jar of flour will not be used up and the jug of oil will not run dry until the day the LORD gives rain on the land" (1 Kings 17:14). He knew the widow was the "faucet" through which God would open the "windows" of heaven.

The principle illustrated here is that when we give in faith, those gifts will be the occasion for God to start his giving. Only when we give do we empty a part of ourselves, making room for God to give through us and more to us!

Her Gift

This woman was both trusting and generous. Using her last bit of flour and oil she baked bread for Elijah, not for herself and her starving son. She fed Elijah first. She gave first, before she cared for herself and her son. And she gave everything. In her gift to Elijah she became a timeless model of giving. She gave no excuses for how poor she was, nor that she was starving, nor that she should care for herself and her son first.

We excuse ourselves from giving with a multitude of reasons. God waits patiently, testing the level of our trust and confidence and our generosity. Will we be like this widow and *first* give him everything we have, knowing that the ultimate goal of our giving is to open the floodgates of heaven? Will we *first* give to him, knowing that our gift is the key that will open the door for God's infinite giving?

God's Gift through Her

Because the woman was both generous and trusting, and because she placed God and his prophet before her own needs, she opened the door of her life so that God's fountains of giving could flow through her. The result? "So there was food every day for Elijah and for the woman and her family. For the jar of flour was not used up and the jug of oil did not run dry" (1 Kings 17:15–16). God does "exceedingly, abundantly, above" (Ephesians 3:20) all we can imagine when we permit him to do it by our giving and through our prayers.

We act on his behalf, and when we fail to give and pray, as his ambassadors, we fail to open the opportunities for God to act through our giving and prayer. There was a need to feed the prophet. She had no resources but flour and oil, enough for one meal. She gave it. God used her gift as an opportunity to pour out his continuing resources. This is the pattern of giving taught over and over again in Scripture. He will multiply both our resources to give more and the effects of our giving.

REFLECTION AND DISCUSSION

1. What did you like the most in this story of the widow's gift?
2. Why was the widow willing to give her last meal to Elijah rather than keep it for her son?
3. How can you apply this lesson in a practical way in your life?

4. Share a time in your life when you felt like the widow. How did God reveal his power to you?

God Protects a Nation through a Shepherd's Gift

As [Goliath] the Philistine moved closer to attack him, David ran quickly toward the battle line to meet him. Reaching into his bag and taking out a stone, he slung it and struck the Philistine on the forehead. The stone sank into his forehead, and he fell facedown on the ground. So David triumphed over the Philistine with a sling and a stone; without a sword in his hand he struck down the Philistine and killed him. (1 Samuel 17:48–50)

The giant blasphemed God and intimidated the army of Israel. The soldiers could see only his size, his armor, his fierce appearance. They failed to see their infinite God. But the little shepherd boy saw. David did not see the giant. All he saw was the size of his God. He looked at God as his resource, and in the light of God's strength he offered to fight the giant, knowing that his gift of himself was God's opportunity to protect his nation. Saul, seeing only human strength, clothed David with his armor. But the human defenses of men only hindered the little shepherd and kept God from acting. He knew that if he gave himself to God, God would give through him to protect not only him but the entire nation. Our giving opens the windows of heaven, enabling God to supernaturally multiply our gifts.

The Need

Israel faced a nine-foot giant who was clothed in armor so heavy a normal man could not lift it. He terrorized Israel daily, taunting them to provide a soldier to engage him in battle, offering that if he was defeated all the Philistine army would become their servants. But if Goliath won, Israel would be the slaves of the Philistines. Every day he shouted his proposition, and not only the soldiers but their king trembled in fear. They had no idea of how to meet this challenge, for they could not see beyond the giant and his armor and their own weakness. Fear kept them from seeing an infinite God who could save them with his unlimited divine power.

Failure to measure life's challenges in the light of God's power and resources is the primary reason for our weakness. We face insurmountable challenges and fail to grasp the promise of 2 Corinthians 10:4: "The weapons we fight with are not the weapons of the world. On the contrary, they have divine power" to face demonic power and threats. When we give and see only the size of our human gift, we are like Saul and the Israelite soldiers who saw Goliath only in the light of their personal weakness. They forgot that when we give, we unlock God's unlimited resources, which will meet any need.

The True Resource

David, the little shepherd boy, listened to the giant. He was incensed by the blasphemy of the giant and by the cowardice of the soldiers. His God was dishonored. And so this little keeper of sheep offered to fight the giant himself. What a commentary on the pathetic lack of faith and trust in God into which Israel had fallen. Under sinful Saul they had completely lost confidence in God and relied only on themselves.

God showed them how ridiculous it is for us to depend on human power. He brought deliverance to them through a little shepherd boy. When we evaluate a need in terms of what we can do about it with our pitiful little resources, rather than turning to God's infinite resources, we always will miss the opportunity of seeing God work supernaturally. He shows his amazing power when the challenge facing us is beyond all human resources. When we give, in spite of the smallness of the gift compared to the overwhelming challenge, we set up an opportunity to see God's multiplying work in meeting the need and resupplying our limited resources.

This truth caused Paul to write, "That is why, for Christ's sake, I delight in weaknesses, in insults, in hardships, in persecutions, in difficulties. For when I am weak, then I am strong" (2 Corinthians 12:10). Paul knew his resources were in the infinite power of God, and the weaker he appeared, the greater was the opening for God to pour his power through him.

David's Gift

With great confidence in God, the little shepherd walked out on the battlefield with only his sling. Goliath was incensed. He was humiliated, and rightly so, that Israel thought so little of him that a shepherd boy without armor or a sword was their choice of a soldier to fight him. It was an insult of the first order.

David did not trust in the strength of man or in the power of armies and soldiers. His mind was filled with his God and in the confidence that if he gave himself, God would fill him with power that was exceedingly, abundantly above all that he could ask or imagine. David did not view giving in a horizontal way, in mere terms of his own strength, but rather he saw his gift vertically as that which would open the door for his God to act.

Is that how we see what we give?

God's Gift

God guided David's hand as he slung the stone into the giant's forehead, sinking it deep in his skull and killing him instantly. God honored David's gift of courage, trust, and sacrifice in placing himself in the face of death. The key to God working in this unusual way was David's total, sacrificial giving of himself. God waits for us to take the first step by trusting him, and the moment we open the way through our giving, he performs his wonders. All believers must learn how to make those first, sacrificial gifts and then God, who worked through David to slay Goliath and worked through the starving widow's gift to feed his prophet, will also work through us in ways we cannot comprehend.

REFLECTION AND DISCUSSION

1. What did you like best in this meditation?
2. What giants do you face in your life?
3. In what ways might God be multiplying some of your gifts?
4. Why is it so hard for us to take the first step of sacrificial giving?

The Fewer Our Resources, the Greater God's Gift

The LORD said to Gideon, "You have too many men for me to deliver Midian into their hands. . . ." (Judges 7:2a)

Could it be that a gift is too big for God? That seems to be the point of the story of Gideon. At first so reluctant, he went on to recruit thirty-two thousand men. But instead of complimenting him on a job well done, God said in effect, *Too many! Israel's strength must always be unquestionably in me.*

Is it possible to have too many resources?

Is it possible that our gifts could be too large? Is it possible that a gift is so great that people cannot see beyond our wealth and generosity to the God who uses our giving as the doorway for his giving? Can our giving block others' view of God by calling attention only to our human wealth and generosity?

Ask yourself this: Is everything about my Christianity explainable in human terms? Are there any inexplicable, surprising events in my walk with Christ? Have I given gifts that bring results far beyond all human explanation?

Or are your gifts merely a reflection of your personal wealth and power?

The Need

Israel had reached an all-time low. Many people were living in caves. At each planting season, the Midianites invaded them, camped on their land, and ruined their crops. Trembling, the Israelites ran to the mountain caves (Judges 6:2). The people of God had fallen into utter disgrace. They brought shame upon the name of God through their weakness and cowardice, a weakness brought about by their idol worship.

Their Resources

Although Gideon had no confidence in himself, God convinced Gideon that he could be used to conquer Israel's enemies. Then, in an about-face, trusting in himself, Gideon recruited soldiers. He depended on his own strength and persuasive powers. For a person who had shown so little leadership ability, the results were staggering. To his surprise thirty-two thousand troops signed up.

Yet God saw a danger in thirty-two thousand soldiers—a danger that Israel would boast about her power by saying that her own strength had saved her. God saw that Israel might believe it was her strength that ensured her safety and not God's. Thirty-two thousand soldiers blocked their view and kept them from seeing what God would do.

We long for the church to be rich and wealthy, but does God? Does God see the same danger that he saw in Israel? If the church finances the spread of the good news through its own resources, will it not boast that it has done it in its own strength? Is it not far better to work with a very poor church, so that when their giving produces miracles of God's provision it will show that God is the infinite source of strength and resources? When we fund churches with our multimillion-dollar gifts and build buildings with human plans like the corporate buildings around us, does it reflect our power, wealth, and wisdom, or God's? When do the things we do have only one explanation: namely, that only God could have done it?

Could this perhaps be one of the reasons why the church often appears to be so weak? Is it because we do so much in our human strength and wealth that it appears that we are helping out a crippled, weak, and poverty-stricken God? Do we give as if God depends on us, or we depend on God? Do our gifts point to us, to our power and wealth, or do they point to God's infinite generosity?

The Gift

Through a series of tests God selected only three hundred soldiers of the original thirty-two thousand soldiers, who were fit to be used. Why did God reject all the others? One of the reasons is that they lacked faith. God eliminated them by saying that anyone who trembled could turn back. Others, at the brook, showed that they lacked readiness. Only three hundred were fit to be used by God.

Here is an important lesson in giving. God used the gift of the widow to feed Elijah. He used the little shepherd boy David to kill the giant. They had something in common. It was something that 31,700 of Gideon's soldiers did not have: an unwavering faith that God would use them far beyond their human abilities. They trusted in themselves, not God. They saw themselves as "helping God out."

As we give our gifts to God we must be pure, always believing that the result will be so great that the only explanation would be God worked a miracle! If the gift points back to us, if what we give can easily be explained only in human terms, then we need to reconsider our giving.

God's Gift

Each of the three hundred soldiers was given a lamp, an empty jar, and a trumpet. That's all it took! Late at night, surrounding the Midianites, they lit their lamps, hid them in jars, and blew their trumpets and smashed the jars. God caused fear and confusion among the enemy soldiers to such an extent that they started to kill each other. They then turned and ran, crying and shouting in dismay.

God is the force that will turn our enemies back, not our wealth or power. It is the way in which our gift is given that unleashes God's infinite giving. Do we trust our own funds and talents to transform the world, or do we see that we are opening the door for God to flow through us with his divine transforming power?

REFLECTION AND DISCUSSION

1. What did you like best in this meditation?
2. Give examples of how we rely on our own resources and not on God.
3. When in your life have you given a gift that pointed to God's power?

Our Giving Causes God to Open the Door

Joshua said to the Israelites, "Come here and listen to the words of the Lord your God. . . . See, the ark of the covenant of the Lord of all the earth will go into the Jordan ahead of you." . . .

So when the people broke camp to cross the Jordan, the priests carrying the ark of the covenant went ahead of them. Now the Jordan is at flood stage all during harvest. Yet as soon as the priests who carried the ark reached the Jordan and their feet touched the water's edge, the water from upstream stopped flowing. (Joshua 3:9,11, 14–16)

The river was at flood stage, turbulent, dangerous, and waiting for its victims. The Israelites, not fond of water to begin with, were petrified. How were they going to get across to the Promised Land? There was no human way, no opening, no bridge, no way around. They were asked to do one thing and only one thing: Their leaders had to get their feet wet. Only if they first got their feet wet would God open the door and part the river.

The Need

God doesn't make it easy, does he? Why couldn't God pick a time when the riverbed was dry, or even when the Jordan went back to being little more than a small creek? Hadn't Israel suffered enough?

God sees things differently than we do. He is always eager to teach us new lessons. God begins this lesson with some of the most wonderful promises in Scripture. He told Joshua, "Do not be discouraged, for the LORD your God will be with you wherever you go" (Joshua 1:9).

Their Resources

The first thing God wants to show in this test is the complete inability of Israel to pass through the flood-swollen stream. Israel, under their leader, had absolutely no resources to overcome this obstacle. How often do we feel the same way? We often feel that the demands on our ministry, the opportunities and open doors for spreading the gospel, are limited only by our lack of resources. At no time in the history of spreading the gospel in India has there ever been more openness, more longing, more receptivity. And yet many people have told me that they do not want to give to India because it is so big and overwhelming they feel they cannot make a dent in it. But God doesn't call us to do it, only to let him do it through our giving and expect the unexpected.

Mission India is a testimony to God's giving through us. In human terms it is among the smallest of the small; a Western agency with less than twenty-five employees at the time of this writing. Yet between 2002 and 2008 the national Indian missions and churches that Mission India serves reported making over one million new disciples *annually* at an average cost of less than $5.00 per disciple as a direct result of this little ministry's training. This is an ongoing testimony not to the ingenuity of man but to the power of God. Here is a movement that defies all human logic. God has touched human giving to multiply it far beyond all we could ask or imagine.

Their Gift

In spite of their total lack of resources, the Israelites had one thing to give—obedience. God asked them to step into the water. Israel had to take the first step, a fearsome step. They had to walk into the Jordan with the ark, not knowing what would happen. It had continued to flow as long as they stood on the bank looking at it and wondering if they would drown. But as the woman gave her only meal, as David gave complete obedience in trusting God, and as Gideon's three hundred soldiers obeyed, so Israel did what God asked. They obeyed. They went forward. They got their feet wet.

And that is what we must do in giving. No matter how poor we might be, we must get our "feet wet" by trusting God and giving him the first gift. We cannot stand back and wait for God to first supply or first open the Jordan River. We must walk in the water before it is parted.

God's Gift

And God parted the river. The water stopped *at a great distance.* Make no mistake about it; God opened the door wide. Not only was the water walled up a great distance upstream, it was completely dry downstream as well. God's gift of parting the river came because of the gift of the priests who in faith stepped in the river before it parted.

We must always be careful when viewing challenges God puts before us, not to fall into the trap of relying on human power. If we view them only in terms of what we can do, we will fail. God did not ask the Israelites to get across by their own resources or by helping themselves. He asked them to trust *him* to get them across and to show that trust by taking the first step into that turbulent water *before the water was parted!*

This is what faith-promise giving is. It is our commitment to God that we will give a certain sum of money for his work. And we have faith that he in turn will provide for us in some unexpected way that reflects his means and not our effort!

A schoolteacher was deeply moved by the challenge of his pastor to give to a certain mission—so moved that he gave $1,000, which he had saved to buy a new cabinet that he had dreamed of for many years. That same night he happened to visit the cabinetmaker whose work he had admired so long. The cabinetmaker then offered, "I'm thinking of making another cabinet, and I don't have room for two of them. You can take this one if you want." God provided the cabinet.

We need the confidence of the little boy who was so moved by the mission challenge that he pledged his entire allowance and then leaned over on his dad's shoulder and said, "Hey, Dad, I need a raise!"

REFLECTION AND DISCUSSION

1. What did you like best in this meditation?
2. What do you need to do first before you can expect God's giving through you?
3. Have you ever pledged "beyond your ability to give?" What happened?

Our Gifts Allow God to Multiply His

Taking the five loaves and the two fish and looking up to heaven, he gave thanks and broke the loaves. Then he gave them to his disciples to set before the people. He also divided the two fish among them all. They all ate and were satisfied, and the disciples picked up twelve basketfuls of broken pieces of bread and fish. The number of the men who had eaten was five thousand. (Mark 6:41–44)

It was late in the day when it happened. Mark tells us there were five thousand men, which means there might have been more than twenty thousand people, counting women and children. Jesus was a popular rabbi. Little wonder the other rabbis were jealous. It was the end of the day and no one had eaten. There were no stores at which they could buy food. What could they do? Jesus asked that the disciples collect any food they could find. All they found were five loaves of bread and two fish—a little boy's lunch.

But when such is given to Christ, it is enough!

The Need

John tells us that Jesus asked the disciples how to feed the crowd, not for information but to test them. "He said this to test [them], for He Himself knew what He would do" (John 6:6 NKJV). God continuously tests us "to see what we will do." He allows staggering needs to be set before us. "How will you feed them?" Christ asks. Of all the pictures of need compared to human resources, this one is probably the most dramatic to be found in Scripture. How does one go about feeding five thousand men, perhaps as many as twenty thousand or more people, without food?

The question Jesus asked of his twelve disciples, "Where shall we buy bread for these people to eat?" (John 6:5) is the question that Christ keeps asking of his followers today. He is asking us, "Where will you get the resources to bring my gospel to everyone, everywhere?" Is our response any different than that of the disciples? Is our situation any more hopeless than that of the Twelve? How can we expect our paltry gifts to bring transformation to India and the nations of the world?

The disciples' response displayed careful calculation based solely on human resources. Their first solution was to send the people away. Let them find their own bread. They have enough money. Let them buy their own food (Mark 6:36). Has this been your response when faced with overwhelming need? How can we possibly provide for all the street children in the world? How can we minister to all the starving poor in the slums? How can we bring education to people who cannot read or write in India? Send them away — let them fend for themselves. Forget about them, for it is hopeless.

But, when Christians fail to respond to the need and horrible spiritual darkness, they miss the opportunity to see the miracles of the Savior! When the need is so staggering that it seems hopeless, we face a great opportunity to see God's resources flow through our meager, ridiculous gifts, beyond "all we can ask or imagine."

Jesus would not accept the answer of the disciples. Instead, he replied, "You give them something to eat" (Mark 6:37). But the disciples, having done their research, replied, "That would take eight months of a man's wages! Are we to go and spend that much on bread and give it to them to eat?" (Mark 6:37).

Their Resources

Jesus told his disciples to search the crowd to find any available food. They returned with only a little boy's small lunch of five barley loaves and two fish (John 6:9). The discovery of this paltry amount of food only increased the skepticism of the disciples. How would five little barley loaves and two fish feed so many people? The little boy didn't insist on keeping one loaf of bread and one fish for himself. He gave everything to Jesus to do with as he wished. The child had no "adult" reservations, but in childlike dependency entrusted his entire lunch to the Savior. In doing this, the little boy depended on Christ and not on the size of his lunch to feed the crowd. Are we willing and ready to do the same? Do we have the faith of a little child to freely give to Jesus all we have?

Christ's Gift

Jesus "organized" the crowd, having them sit on the grass in groups of hundreds and fifties so that they could be better served. Christ took the five little loaves and two fish and, looking to heaven, gave thanks to his Father. He divided the fish and bread and distributed food to the entire crowd.

What a picture of the way Christ works through our gifts. Who could imagine that five loaves and two fish would feed thousands? When we open the windows of heaven through our sacrificial gifts, God not only multiplies the results to those who receive the gifts but also multiplies our resources to give more. Two fish and five little loaves of bread were multiplied to feed thousands of people and twelve basketfuls of food were left over—far more than they started with!

He started with two fish and five loaves of bread. All were fed. And twelve baskets were left over! Remember this the next time you give!

REFLECTION AND DISCUSSION

1. What did you like best in this meditation?
2. How can you apply this to your own life?
3. What prevents you from having a childlike trust that God will multiply your gifts?
4. When in your life have you felt inadequate to respond to an overwhelming need? Would you respond differently today?

We Give God's Power

When [a crippled man] saw Peter and John about to enter, he asked them for money. Peter looked straight at him, as did John. Then Peter said, "Look at us!" So the man gave them his attention, expecting to get something from them.

Then Peter said, "Silver or gold I do not have, but what I have I give you. In the name of Jesus Christ of Nazareth, walk." Taking him by the right hand, he helped him up, and instantly the man's feet and ankles became strong. (Acts 3:3–7)

India has millions of them. You will find them on the street corners, tapping on the car windows, peering through the windshields, pleading with the occupants for a handout. They line the entrances to churches and temples, holding out leprous stumps, peering with mutilated faces, tugging at the emotions. Most are organized and owned by beggar masters, and many have been intentionally crippled and mutilated. These are the beggars of India. There are too many to help. What can we do with our limited resources?

We can remember Peter's words: "What I have I give you."

The Need

He was crippled from birth. He had never walked or known the dignity of work. He was like India's teeming millions of street and temple beggars. He called out to Peter and John that day. There was nothing new in that, for that was his daily occupation. He was as familiar to them as they were to him. He was there every day and so were Peter and John. But something was different today.

Prior to that day the two seldom noticed him. They had seen beggars before and they had seen him before. I wonder if they remembered the conversation with

Jesus a year earlier. The twelve disciples had observed a beggar born blind one day (John 9:1–12), and rather than being moved with compassion they made him the subject of an argument. "Who was responsible for the sin that made this man blind?" they inquired of Jesus, "This man or his parents?"

Christ rebuked them by telling them that such questions were wrong. This blind man was not there to be the subject of a religious discussion or argument. He was not there to be judged as to whether he or his parents had sinned. The man was blind, he said, so that the Father's glory might be seen in him. Thereupon, the Savior healed the man, revealing his power.

Christ corrects our vision of the dark spots of life by calling us to look at each tragedy in the light of how the Father might show his glory through it. A Russian proverb says, "The darker the night, the brighter the light." In our lives, the darker the problem the greater the miracle when Christ uses the darkness as an opportunity to show his glory and power. Perhaps Peter and John had learned from this lesson and now noticed the beggar and listened to his call. They saw the need. And they knew they had nothing of human resources (silver and gold) to give the beggar.

The Resources
It was obvious, of course, that they had no silver and gold to give. They were still poor. There are those who claim that Christ's followers will be blessed with material prosperity if only they learn how to give. However, when we give as just another way of getting, giving becomes merely another form of selfishness. God will not usually bless giving that is motivated by personal gain. When Christians are blessed with additional material gifts because they gave, the reason is that they are being enabled to give more. The new wealth entrusted to them is not for their selfish enjoyment but to be given to meet others' needs! Peter and John had not yet reached the point where they had material resources to give to help this man. They had nothing.

The Real Gift

Peter dignified the man in Christ's name. "Peter looked straight at him, as did John. Then Peter said, 'Look at us!'" (Acts 3:4). The man had been taught to keep his head down indicating his lowly position, but now tentatively he looked up at them expecting a coin or two in his cup. But what he heard next was the most amazing statement he had ever heard: "Silver and gold I do not have, but what I have I give you. In the name of Jesus Christ of Nazareth, walk" (Acts 3:6). Peter and John, along with all believers, are entrusted with the supernatural power of Christ. In this case it expressed itself in the miracle of healing. It is a power that expresses itself in a multitude of ways, but always with one purpose of bringing glory and attention to the Lord Jesus Christ.

Whenever we pray for specific needs of others we are claiming the power of Christ for the transformation of their lives. When we B.L.E.S.S. them, praying for the health of their *b*odies, their *l*abor, their *e*ducation and emotions, their *s*ocial relationships, and their *s*piritual life in Christ, we are calling upon the power of Christ to work miracles. We are giving what we have, namely, supernatural power to meet daily needs. Reflect on the seven gifts the Savior gives so that we might give them to others (week 2). This is what Peter gave to the beggar. As we pray and back up our prayers with caring and sharing, we give the greatest gift of all: the gift of the person, provision, power, protection, resurrection, reign, and return of Jesus Christ.

God's power flowed, and the man was healed. Join Peter and John in giving what we have, namely, the infinite resources of our Savior!

REFLECTION AND DISCUSSION

1. What did you like best in this meditation?
2. What gifts have you given, like Peter and John, that reflect the power of Christ?

Giving Our All Is All Christ Desires

As he looked up, Jesus saw the rich putting their gifts into the temple treasury. He also saw a poor widow put in two very small copper coins. "I tell you the truth," he said, "this poor widow has put in more than all the others. All these people gave their gifts out of their wealth; but she out of her poverty put in all she had to live on." (Luke 21:1–4)

How much does the gift cost you? The poor widow dropped in a few coins, a few pennies in the offering box. The coins had little value, but it was all she had, all she owned. She had nothing left for food. Everything was gone; she had given all. The rich gave much, but the much was little, for they had so much more. As Jesus watched he said that God does not measure the amount given, but measures the cost of the gift to the giver instead. What is the cost of your gifts? The cost of your gift is an expression of the depth of your love.

Giving is the key that unlocks the windows to the storehouse of God's resources. We have seen overwhelming needs, which make human resources seem paltry and weak in comparison. We have seen people acting with confidence in God as they give their tiny gifts, and God used the gifts as an opportunity to open the windows of heaven and release his infinite resources.

If God is to be honored by the gift, the gift must be significant to the giver. It must be costly. Those who give out of their wealth, as large as the gift might be, and yet have not in any way altered their lifestyle, have not expressed love and honor to God as much as the widow who gave all of her meager belongings. Sacrificial giving is the way in which we say, "I love you."

Years ago, when I was very poor, I happened to glance in the front window of a jewelry store as I walked by. I saw a woman's ring. It had two opals, mounted side by side, symbolizing the love between husband and wife. I stopped, turned, and entered the store. I looked at it and knew that I had to have that ring even though its cost was far beyond anything that I could afford at the time. Without hesitation I bought it, had it gift wrapped, and took it home. I gave the package to my wife and she looked puzzled. "What's this for?" she asked. It was not Christmas. It was not a wedding anniversary. It was not her birthday.

I stumbled a bit as I tried to explain and finally said, "It's a 'for-nothing' gift. I bought it just because I love you and wanted to tell you that. The occasion for this gift, if you need one, is our love for each other."

"I love you" was the occasion for the widow's gift. Her love for God prompted her to give all she had. Jesus watched as the rich gave out of their wealth and this poor widow gave all she had. True giving, he observed, is measured not by the amount of the gift but rather by the cost of the gift to the giver. God does not need giant amounts of money. He is independently wealthy and is not breathlessly waiting for us to help him out. Rather, he prefers our gifts to cost something and thus tell of our love for him.

In a sense, it is easier for the poor to give. They never give out of abundance; they don't have an abundance of money. Every gift costs them dearly. There is a story of a poor man who regularly gave one tenth of all he earned. When he earned one hundred dollars per day it was not difficult for him to give ten dollars to his Lord. When his daily wage doubled to two hundred dollars per day, he still found it easy to give twenty dollars daily as his gift to the Lord. But when he made one million dollars per year he found it very difficult to give one hundred thousand dollars per year. He gave, but *the proportion* of his gift went down. People thought him generous, because the amount of money he gave was large. But it was no longer a tenth of his income. He was not tithing as he did when he was poor.

Is this why God so delights in the gifts of the poor? Is it because they are so much more costly and hence so much more precious to him? We must never excuse ourselves from giving because we are poor. The majority of biblical examples of giving are the gifts of the poor: the starving widow who fed Elijah, the little boy's lunch that Jesus used to feed five thousand. *It is not the amount of the gift that expresses our love so much as the cost of the gift to us.*

Six days before Christ's crucifixion, Mary and Martha and Lazarus gave a special dinner in honor of the Savior. During the dinner Mary expressed her love with a gift that cost a year's wages. She opened a large bottle of the most costly perfume she could buy. She poured it over Jesus' feet and then wiped his feet with her hair. The house was filled with the fragrance of the perfume. In that day and culture this was a profound act of pure love.

There were two interpretations of this act. Judas, the traitor, saw the act only in terms of money. Here was a sizeable sum, a year's wages, wasted in one act. Nothing came of it; to use it this way was a waste. Jesus saw the gift, however, as he saw the gift of the widow's few coins. It was a costly gift speaking to him of Mary's sacrificial love. It's not how much we give, but the proportion of the gift compared to what we have left that tells our love for Christ.

We open the door to God's resources with our costly gifts. Our gifts are the key that unlocks God's miraculous supply and causes it to pour out. We must never treat God as someone who is very poor and needs our gifts. Praise God for poverty, which forces us to rely on God's infinite resources to be released through our gift. As the widow gave, God released his resources and continued to supply flour and oil, enabling her to continue to give. Every one of the stories we have studied this week illustrates Malachi 3:10. Through our giving we open the windows of heaven, releasing showers of blessings that enable us to increase our gifts and bless the recipients of our gifts. The gift that costs the most is the most pleasing to God. It is not the amount, for God is the one who multiplies; it is the price we pay to give.

The third reason for giving is that our giving releases God's infinite giving!

REFLECTION AND DISCUSSION

1. What kind of gifts most honor the Lord?
2. What gift could you give to God that would cost you the most?
3. Why do we tend to focus more on the size of a gift than the cost?

We Give Because Our Giving Enables Others to Give

Not only does our giving enable God to open the windows of heaven and pour blessings on us that we cannot contain, but our giving also enables the recipients of our gifts to give. In a sense all our giving must be like spiritual well drilling. Our gifts must start headwaters of new rivers of living waters.

There are two "greats" in the Bible: the Great Commission, and the Great Commandment. The Great Commission is Christ's final instruction to us to go into all the world and make disciples (Matthew 28:19-20). The Great Commandment defines disciples as those who love for Christ's sake (Matthew 22:37-39). Disciples follow the example of the Savior by loving God above all else, and loving their neighbors as themselves. Disciples are not self-oriented, seeking salvation only because they want to protect themselves from hell and assure their eternal heaven. Disciples have new natures characterized by generosity. Each time we give and make a new disciple or encourage someone who already is a disciple, we are enabling others to give. Making a disciple is spiritual well drilling.

Recently Mission India had an independent research team determine how much longterm reproduction of disciples and churches was occurring. In other words, how many churches (praying, caring communities) were the original churches starting, and how many disciples were the original disciples making? How well were the new spiritual wells producing? In the Institute of Community Transformation Training Program, Indian believers are trained to bring transformation to neighborhoods through planting ongoing, multiplying, worshiping communities. They surveyed 179 graduates who planted 516 churches across India and determined that 89 percent of the churches planted were growing and reproducing on average 3.6 new churches within three years. They found that for every new disciple that had fallen away, an average of seven new disciples had been gained. Disciples are reproducing entities. They express the love of God by forming new communities showing the "new" and radical sacrificial love of the Savior. This week we will examine ways to inspire those to whom we give to multiply our gift by their giving.

We Give in an Equal Exchange Relationship

When a Samaritan woman came to draw water, Jesus said to her, "Will you give me a drink?" (His disciples had gone into the town to buy food.) The Samaritan woman said to him, "You are a Jew and I am a Samaritan woman. How can you ask me for drink?" (For Jews do not associate with Samaritans.) (John 4:7–9)

We sat all day in the conference discussing the dangers of creating dependency through our giving. There was only one national leader from India in the group; all the rest of us were from America. At the end of the day the Indian leader added a startling cultural perspective on things: He had heard much that day about the danger of creating dependency, but dependency in the Indian culture is a virtue, not a vice. The great virtue is "mutual dependency."

The great problem with the West is the fact that we are so self-sufficient and so independent. When giving, we seem to be more interested in feeling good than in creating ways the recipients of our gifts can give. We need more dependency on each other. Our families are breaking down because we worship independence and fail to value dependency upon each other. We do not realize that dependency is the glue of relationships. *Love is mutual dependency and mutual giving.*

Our lone Indian leader went on to point out that dependency in the Indian culture is different than "parasitism." A parasite sucks out for itself without returning anything of value. This is radically different than dependency in which two people are knit together in mutual dependence and mutual giving. God made us to be dependent on him and on each other.

Amazingly God himself chooses to make some of his actions dependent on ours—he will even limit his activity at times to our prayers and our giving. As God gives to us we are to respond in giving our all to him. And as we give to God he in turn is released to give more to us. As others give to us we are to respond by giving to them. They in turn are released to give in return. We are to create communities characterized by the statement, "I don't know what I would have done without you." We need each other. As I help you, you in turn help me.

A version of the wisdom of this Indian leader is found in a secular book by Milton and Rose Friedman, *Free to Choose*. They develop the concept of the "exchange of equal value," which amounts to mutual dependency. The more I've reflected on the concept of an exchange of equal value, the more I understood a basic flaw in much of Western Christian giving. *The greatest gift we can give is to ask people to give.* True giving enables and motivates others to give.

God created us to enter into a mutually dependent relationship with him. He gave the world to Adam and Eve but in return asked Adam and Eve to give their "world" to him; namely their love and obedience by not eating of the Tree of Knowledge of Good and Evil. When God gave the world to Adam and Eve he was putting himself in a relationship of mutual dependency with his image bearers. He was saying, "I'll give you the world if you will care for it on my behalf. I will give you the world if you will give yourself to be my obedient rulers over it." There was in a sense something of an "equal exchange": I'll depend on you and you depend on me. I'll give all to you if you give your all to me. I'll give you the world on condition you in turn live in obedience to my command and freely love me.

This was what the fall all came down to: Adam and Eve refused to obey; they wanted merely to receive, not to give. They gave nothing in return for all of God's gifts to them and thus became parasites, and parasitism always results in death. Receiving without giving destroys.

Christian giving that does not encourage equal exchange is degrading. Any giving that is not mutual degrades. Government welfare programs breed generations of parasites by their failure to demand a mutual exchange. Such programs seldom produce creative, dignified, giving human beings. As rivers of life flow from us we must be certain that we dignify others by having new rivers of life spring up from those who receive our gifts. A disciple is not a self-centered seeker of truth, or a person wanting an eternal "fire insurance policy" to ensure entrance to glory, but rather a source of giving torrents of love. When we make a new disciple we drill a new well of giving!

Christ's request of help from the Samaritan woman, recorded in John 4:7, is astounding: "Jesus said to her, 'Will you give me a drink?'" He nearly blew her off the well with his request. Jews never went into Samaria, yet Jesus "had to go into Samaria." No Jewish man would talk to a Samaritan woman. No rabbi would ever ask a Samaritan woman (an untouchable) for a drink of water. In that request for a drink of water, Jesus was giving an incredible gift—one that I doubt had ever been given to this woman. It was the gift of dignity. It was an offer to exchange something of value: her water for his water.

One of the quickest ways to spread the gospel is by asking a non-Christian to help you in your ministry of love and assistance to those who are hurting in the neighborhood. Doing so, you allow them to experience the joy of participating with you in giving to others, and the Lord is the one who in response will open their hearts to receive him. We can easily cripple converts with our cash if we unwisely make them dependent on our continued giving.

Reflect on week 1 for a moment. We learned that being born again was being changed from a stagnant pond to a flowing river. Remember how that river of Ezekiel 47 increased so miraculously? Now you can see the reason for that increase. When we give we enable both God and others to join in our giving. As those three streams merge — our giving, God's giving, and others' giving — torrents of living water flood out through our gifts.

Our giving is to result in *mutual* dependency.

REFLECTION AND DISCUSSION

1. Share and discuss instances where giving has resulted in "parasitism."
2. Reflect on your concept of discipleship. Is it being changed? If so, how?
3. In what practical ways will you change your giving patterns?

Our Giving Must Make Giving Disciples

And anyone who does not take up his cross and follow me is not worthy of me. Whoever finds his life will lose it, and whoever loses his life for my sake will find it. (Matthew 10:38–39)

Jesus asks of us who would be worthy to follow him that we in turn crucify ourselves and give our lives for him (Matthew 16:24–26). And as we give to make disciples we not only open the windows of heaven, but we also open up the lives of those who become disciples to be rivers of life. Our giving in missions enables both God and others to give in new and different ways they were not giving before.

When we "accept" the gift of salvation we are, according to our Savior's own words, engaging in the ultimate exchange of value by giving up our life in return for his giving up his life for us. We not only give up our life for him but for each other. All four of the gospel writers refer to this as mutual cross bearing or crucifixion. The first three gospels each repeat the "spiritual exchange" formula. Jesus died for us; thus we must die (take up our cross) for him. As Jesus gave his life for us, so we must in turn give our life for him (Matthew 10:38).

John gives us an exact definition of how a relationship with Christ is a mutually dependent relationship, a relationship of total surrender to each other: "As I have loved you, so you must love one another. By this all men will know that you are my disciples, if you love one another" (John 13:34–35).

We have distorted the saving relationship with Christ in two ways, often rendering the modern, Western church impotent and irrelevant. First when we present salvation not as a mutual giving between Jesus and ourselves but solely in terms of Jesus' gift to us, we create a welfare society of spiritual parasites. Christianity becomes a one-way street of God's giving to us. All we need do to be saved is to accept Christ's offer. We fail to dignify people when we fail to present the mutual giving formula on which all relationships are built. Many of the presentations of the gospel are little more than a call to spiritual parasitism. Church membership is determined not on the basis of which church offers us the best way to serve Christ but rather on the basis of which church best serves our spiritual needs. We love quoting Ephesians 2:8–9 but forget verse 10. God redeemed us for the purpose of doing good works—good works that were planned for us before the world began.

Second, when we do give, we seem to give primarily for our own benefit, for our own programs and for our own buildings. Our giving is first of all directed toward our own comfort and pleasure. Statistics showing the charities to which Christians give, compiled by David Barrett in the

Encyclopedia of World Christianity, indicate that ninety-seven cents of each dollar given to the church is directed toward maintaining its own program, not making new disciples. When we give, our giving is too often confined to maintaining our religion. Furthermore, Western Christians, who represent today only one third of the Christians in the world, own 85 percent of all Christian wealth.

Robert Lewis, in his book *The Church of Irresistible Influence*, points out that today six out of ten Americans believe the church is irrelevant. This is partly because they see that "not only is our giving down to a trickle (only about two percent of our income on average) but the giving is directed inward for our own programs and comfort, which is one of the primary reasons Christianity has virtually no impact on our culture" (p. 23).

Contrast the supernatural impact on society that the early clusters of believers had on the pagan Roman Empire, or that those Jewish Christians had in Jerusalem in the very early days following Pentecost as the church exploded from three thousand individuals on the first day to an additional five thousand extended families shortly thereafter (Acts 4:4). The followers of Jesus were elevated to a new sense of dignity by Christ's call to follow his example of total sacrifice for each other, and they expressed it in a radically different kind of concern for the poor (Acts 2:42–47). It was a different concern than had ever been experienced in the culture of that time, and God used Christians' sacrificial giving for the poor to explosively spread the gospel.

When Jesus told the rich man that inheriting the kingdom of God meant entering a relationship of mutual sacrifice, the man rejected it and turned away (Mark 10:21-23). The rich young man was not interested in giving everything to the poor. He was devoted to getting, not giving, and when he found that the kingdom of heaven was made up of those who had been born again to give he was not interested. He was interested only in getting more, not giving more. Whenever the gospel is presented with the dignifying, biblical challenge of giving, the gospel explodes; when the gospel is presented merely in terms of a one-way gift, people yawn.

The specific goal in the Great Commission is to make disciples, and Christ defines disciples as people who have been born again to be rivers of new love. A disciple is a producer. A disciple gives. A disciple is a fruit bearer (John 15:1–5). Jesus gives pagans the right to judge whether those who claim to follow him are his disciples by the love they show to each other and to the world (John 13:14, 35). Making disciples means enabling, motivating, and teaching people to give!

We must never separate the Great Commission from the Great Commandment. The Great Commission is to make disciples and the Great Commandment is the explanation of the Great Commission: namely, that discipleship is a relationship of the exchanging of love. Disciples are those who, in response to the love of Christ, are giving love to one another and to their neighbors. So how much would your river increase if you measured your giving by the number of new rivers you had started?

REFLECTION AND DISCUSSION

1. In the light of the multitude of over-whelming needs in India, how do you justify making disciples as the first task of the church?
2. How is making disciples the foremost way of meeting India's many needs?
3. Have you, or has your church, ever measured the number of disciples you have made or are making?
4. Have you ever set a goal for the number of new disciples you want to make? What would be the advantage of this kind of goal setting?

A Systematic, Measurable Increase in Giving

Nevertheless, more and more men and women believed in the Lord and were added to their number. (Acts 5:14)

Mission India describes their ministry as a systematic and measurable method of making disciples. The New Testament shows how Paul worked in a systematic and measurable way and within ten years had planted "starter" churches in every major region. Christ's instructions to the seventy-two were to systematically and measurably go to every village: "After this the Lord appointed seventy-two others and sent them two by two ahead of him to every town and place where he was about to go" (Luke 10:1).

The principle of moving systematically and measurably does not mean, however, that we spend great amounts of time training people. We must never stifle disciple making by misleading people to think that they must first be trained in order to witness. This mission principle is one of the primary principles taught by Roland Allen in his book *The Spontaneous Expansion of the Church*. He writes, "It ought to be a cardinal principle with missionaries that anyone who knows enough to be saved by Christ knows enough to tell another how he may be saved" (p. 54).

Many graduates of Bible colleges and seminaries get turned inward and find the flow of their river slowed or stopped as they become degree oriented rather than oriented toward making disciples. The moment someone comes to Christ, the flow of the "rivers of living water" must be released. They must start disciple making immediately, and in the process of witnessing they are being trained.

Mission India teaches the Indian leaders and evangelists the basic principles of how to reach families, illiterates, and children with the gospel. Then they must *immediately* put these principles into practice by giving what they have learned to others. And they must be accountable through proper reporting. They don't merely sit in seminars and receive; full learning includes practice and implementation.

One of the measurable and systematic goals to which Mission India holds its partners accountable is the goal of saturating specific geographic areas (villages and towns) with prayer cells so that every family in the area can be prayed for personally. Each new disciple commits to pray the B.L.E.S.S. prayer daily for five families. Disciples meet weekly (often daily) in a prayer cell for worship and accountability. This systematic, measurable approach to making new disciples works in any country.

The B.L.E.S.S. prayer is based on the story of Jesus' transformation of a leper, recorded in Matthew 8:1–4. (See *Why Pray?* the first book in this series.) In this short but dramatic account, a leper approached Christ and asked that he be made clean. Christ reached out and touched the man. With the touch of the Savior, the man went through five transformations. His body was healed of leprosy. Because his body was transformed he could go back to work—his labor was transformed. Because both his body and labor were transformed he was transformed emotionally—he had joy. And through these three transformations his social life was transformed—he no longer was an outcast. The leper experienced these four external transformations because there was an internal transformation—spiritual life in Christ. This new spiritual life in Christ transformed his body, labor, emotions, and social life.

Each disciple of Jesus should join in a systematic and measurable plan of having every family in a specific area B.L.E.S.S.ed daily. Every city should be a city of H.O.P.E. (homes of prayer every day) with a systematic, accountable plan to plant houses of prayer at the rate of one for every twenty-five residences, and to offer to meet all practical needs as channels of the answers to their prayers. The H.O.P.E. plan is a simple, four-step plan for total transformation of an area, such as a neighborhood, village, apartment complex, condo complex, or mobile home park based on Revelation 3:20: "Here I am! I stand at the door and knock. If anyone hears my voice and opens the door, I will come in and eat with him, and he with me."

The first step is to realize who is standing at the door of your home and neighborhood. It is Jesus, whose presence is the opposite of all evil. Christ tells us in Matthew 18:20 that he will be present where two or more are gathered in prayer. To bring Christ's presence into a neighborhood is the very first step in transformation.

The second step is forming a welcoming committee consisting of two or more people, for no one can bring Christ in alone, according to Matthew 18:20. The third step is to pry open the door through prayer walking, caring for neighbors, and building relationships. The fourth step is to form a "2:42" ongoing praying, caring community. (Read Acts 2:42 to find out how Jerusalem was transformed through little caring and worshiping groups in homes.)

When you read the accounts Luke kept of the growth of the New Testament church, it is clear Luke was accountable. He believed in and reported measurable and systematic growth. Our giving must be accountable and systematic. We must not give based on emotions but on careful consideration of how Christ's Great Commission is being carried out through our gifts. Are disciples being made? Are churches being planted? Or, are our funds going into programs that have little relationship to systematic, measurable making of disciples?

REFLECTION AND DISCUSSION

1. Is your giving systematic and measurable?
2. What are you "getting" for your giving dollar? Are you starting new rivers of giving?
3. What are some ways in which we can hold each other accountable for growth?

You Don't Need Much to Start New Rivers of Giving

Do not take a purse or bag or sandals; and do not greet anyone on the road. When you enter a house, first say, "Peace to this house." If a man of peace is there, your peace will rest on him; if not, it will return to you. Stay in that house, eating and drinking whatever they give you. (Luke 10:4–7)

The boredom of the youth group that day back in 1967 was exceeded only by my boredom as I led them. It was an epidemic of boredom, and I felt I needed to do something dramatic as a young pastor to spark the teens' attention. And so, with little forethought, I asked them if they had ever seen a miracle, to which they replied with continued boredom that they had not.

I then asked them if they believed in miracles, which resulted in a slight increase in interest and participation, and they all mildly agreed that maybe God could work miracles. I moved on. "How many of you would like to see a miracle?" That got their attention.

"But do we get to see a miracle?" they asked.

I said, "One thing is certain. God won't do a miracle unless you ask him to."

"What do you have in mind?" they pressed.

"Well, we need to build a church in Taiwan; and that will cost $10,000. Why don't you ask God to raise that money through your efforts?" They all started to laugh. This was 1967 when, as a young pastor my entire salary was only about $7,000. Today it would be something like asking a group of thirty teens if they thought God could raise $80,000 through them. They talked about it a little and agreed: They wanted to see God work a miracle of raising $10,000 through them for a church in Taiwan.

"What do we do to raise all this money?" they asked, to which I replied, "How do I know what to do? This is supposed to be a miracle. If I knew what to do it would not be a miracle. I do know what you should *not* be doing—I don't want you going through the congregation asking for great big sums of money. I have a hard enough time raising the church budget without having a bunch of teens messing around with the giving patterns. What I will let you do, however, is place a bank in every home in the church and collect loose change—pennies, nickels, dimes, quarters, and (back in those days) half dollars."

They laughed again. "Collect $10,000 with pennies, nickels, dimes, and quarters? That would take forever."

"If you have a better idea, let's do it; but for now that seems to be the best we can come up with. So, each of you take on a few families, bring a bank to them, and tell them to put loose change in it, and you will collect it once a month for the coming year. Let's see what happens."

The young people took a bank to every family in the church and a month later called back on all the families to pick up the loose change. They were amazed that it took over two-and-a-half hours to count out $2,500 in loose change. In the first month they were one quarter of the way.

They collected loose change monthly for the next ten months. While we had agreed to do it for twelve months, by the end of the ten months they had collected not $10,000 but $12,500, and much to our surprise, every fund in the church also had a surplus. We were overwhelmed at God's miracle of multiplying loose change to a sum the church would never have agreed to raise.

It started with so little, but God multiplied it in three ways. First, the total was far more than we ever dreamed. We would have been happy with $10,000, which was in itself unheard of; but to raise $12,500—that was beyond any expectation.

The second startling thing that happened was the fact that as the families collected their loose change they actually started giving more to the church as well. Our overall giving increased significantly that year.

The third result, however, was the most startling; and I did not find out about it until thirty years later. We provided our denominational mission board with the funds they needed to build a church in downtown Taipei. None of us ever had the opportunity to go to Taiwan and see the church, and we soon forgot about that building. One day, years later, my wife and I were having coffee with a missionary from Taiwan, and I asked what had happened to the church we paid for.

He thought for a moment and said, "Church? What church?" I was a little concerned and told him the story of how years ago we had raised the money to build a church. He started to laugh. "Didn't you hear what happened?" he said. "That was torn down because the value of the property had risen so high. Your funds paid for the initial building, but now there is a high rise on your land. The church meets on the ground floor, mission offices are on the next three floors, and the rest is apartments that are rented out for continuing income for the mission efforts!"

My wife and I were stunned. The church in Taiwan had taken our little gift and multiplied it. God multiplies our giving, both directly through increased resources, but also through the way the gift enables others to give. A loose-change offering was multiplied in so many ways.

Jesus told the seventy-two not to take any money with them. They were to depend on those to whom they were sent for food and lodging. Their gift of bringing Christ was to result in encouraging others to give. Christ's directions to the seventy-two are stunning: Don't greet anyone along the way but be single minded, and systematic; do not be side-tracked; and when you get to the houses of peace, make certain that you immediately motivate them to give by allowing them to feed and house you; don't worry about finance—you will find it on the field. Just do it! How much could we advance missions if we took the Savior's words literally and looked to the field for more financing?

Today, through gifts in kind, approximately one third of Mission India's budget is contributed by the "poor" Indian Christians. God touches and uses that "little" amount, multiplying it beyond imagination. When asked what the Indian leaders like about the program, they say it is the fact that they are making such a great contribution that they feel the program is theirs, not some Western program imposed on them. They have been dignified through the requirements that we have laid down for their giving.

REFLECTION AND DISCUSSION

1. Have you ever used something like loose change to start rivers of giving? If so, how? And what were the results?
2. Why are "little" gifts so important?

A Small Gift Starts
a Family Giving

*Taking the five loaves and the two fish
and looking up to heaven, he gave thanks
and broke them. Then he gave them to the
disciples to set before the people. They all
ate and were satisfied, and the disciples
picked up twelve basketfuls of broken
pieces that were left over.* (Luke 9:16–17)

It is hard to find a story more spectacular
than this story of thousands being fed
by two fish and five loaves of bread with
the result of twelve basketfuls of broken
pieces left over. We have studied it in a
previous meditation, but the following
story graphically illustrates how Christ

multiples a little gift. In this story we see how a gift of $30 spreads out to transform a family and four other neighborhoods.

Selvi was a poor, untouchable mother of four, living in a slum in north Madras, a city now called Chennai, in the southern Indian state of Tamil Nadu. Her slum was not as bad as some, where houses are made of pieces of tin with roofs of blue tarps, but it was very poor nonetheless. Her little, one-room, concrete-block house was without running water or any sewage facilities and was home for six people. Her kitchen stove consisted of three stones in a corner to hold her only cooking pot over the little fire that had no chimney or outside ventilation.

Selvi was constantly, deeply depressed, often sitting in the gloomy darkness of her little windowless home for hours without moving. The sewage flowing freely in the gutter past her front door filled the air with an awful stench. Her husband beat her regularly for losing money to the crooked produce vendors in the market-place. Since she could neither read nor count, she was easy prey for being short-changed. Selvi, like most of the women in the slum, was totally illiterate; she could not add or subtract, or even read the bus signs. Inability to read those signs kept her at home. She feared getting lost since she didn't know what bus to take where she wanted to go or to get back home from wherever she went.

Because she had never gone to school, she did not value education and let her four children run wild through the slum, without going to school. They were dirty, unkempt, and smelly kids. Selvi dreaded her husband's anger the most. It boiled up daily in beatings. Every time she went to market she would be cheated and her husband would lose his temper, often pummeling her and tossing her around. Life was pure misery.

One day a group of actors came to the slum and put on a skit about two kinds of blindness: one kind was curable, but the other was incurable. One person carried a white cane and walked up to a bus stop. Another person who did not appear to be blind was standing there. The blind man asked that person to tell him when bus nine came, but the person refused, saying that he could not read and thus couldn't tell which bus was number nine.

The actors then told the audience of mostly women that there are two kinds of blindness: one curable, the other not. Physical blindness cannot be reversed, but the blindness of not being able to read could be overcome. When people can read they can tell which bus to get on and where to go. When people can read they will no longer be cheated in the market-place. When people can read their income will rise dramatically and their health will improve, for they will know many things about preventing sickness.

The actors then encouraged the ladies to enroll in a class that would teach them how to read and write. It would meet five nights a week for an entire year. It was a big commitment, but they assured the women that they would never be the same again.

Selvi listened and for the first time she had a glimmer of hope. When her husband came home that night she shared the story of the skit and her desire to learn how to read and write and add and subtract. Much to her amazement her husband agreed that she should attend the classes, and so she enrolled.

She learned fast and within two months could add and subtract. She was eager to go to the market and catch the vendors trying to cheat her by giving her the wrong change. When her husband came home that first night after market, she showed him the right change and glowed with pride as he praised her for finally knowing how to add and subtract. Motivated by her new appreciation of the benefits of being able to read and write, she insisted on cleaning up the four boys, combing and oiling their hair, and making certain that they went to school each day and did their lessons.

During the first three months Selvi learned many practical lessons in health, hygiene, and diet. She was amazed that the chronic diarrhea that plagued the family stopped as a result of knowing how to keep her family clean.

Each day, at the bottom of the literacy primer for that day, there was a saying. At first Selvi didn't know where these little sayings were coming from, but she was very intrigued by them. Her teacher told Selvi that these sayings were from a religious book called the Bible. She wanted to know more, and her teacher, who was now her friend and confidant, explained the radically different message of this new book—that there is only one God. "This God loves us so much that he sent his own Son into the world to save us," she told Selvi.

Selvi gave her life to Jesus and immediately started giving. She shared the good news with her husband and her family, and they joined her in believing in Jesus. Now able to read, she gathered the family together each night and read the verse that was at the bottom of the lesson the previous day. They sang the songs and prayed the prayers and they experienced a new joy and happiness.

After about six months Selvi learned how to sew, and she received a free sewing machine from the government. She set up a little tailoring shop and started to supplement her husband's meager income.

Suddenly they had money. (The average income of the newly literate like Selvi goes up 57 percent in the first year of literacy.) They learned to do two things with the money—to save and to give. The ladies in the literacy class started a community "bank" and each one put in a few rupees each week and then loaned the money to class members to help them start a business. The repayment schedule was strictly enforced!

But most of all, Selvi grew rapidly in her faith in Jesus and told the class about how her prayer group at her home was expanding and how some neighbors had joined in their worship. Some of her classmates attended and then three of them started three more prayer cells, so there were four little "house churches" in and around the slum.

Selvi's transformation consisted of two parts; the first was receiving salvation in Christ and the second was in giving the good news of salvation to others. Paul hinted at these two parts to transformation, receiving and giving, in Philemon 6: "I pray that you may be active in sharing your faith, so that you will have *a full under-standing of every good thing we have in Christ.*"

I will never forget Selvi's face as we got to the end of the interview. She glowed as she radiated joy, saying, "And now I have two loves. My Savior Jesus loves me, and now my husband also loves me. I never knew I could be so happy."

All this was accomplished with a gift of $30 that started Selvi giving: A mother was lifted out of depression; four children were enrolled in school and education is changing their lives; health came to the family through new knowledge of diet and hygiene; a love relationship between husband and wife started and wife abuse stopped; family income went up over 57 percent in the first year; the entire family became productive disciples of Christ; a small neighborhood worshiping group was formed; and then three more worship-ing groups were formed.

For the price of a meal for two in a restaurant in the West, Selvi's whole family and many neighbors were transformed for time and eternity! For merely $30, six new spiritual wells producing torrents of living water started to flow from Selvi's family. It will take eternity to unravel how those rivers increased from that one little gift of $30. I wonder if, just perhaps, that thirty-dollar gift might be a greater story than the five loaves and two fish.

Reflection and Discussion

1. Discuss: Will Jesus show us in heaven the extent of the rivers of giving that flowed from our lives on earth?
2. What did you like the most in this story?
3. What is most important—the number of people you can transform through your gifts or the number of temporary possessions you can get to make your life comfortable? What does your giving pattern say about your priorities?

A Slave Set Free

The Spirit of the Sovereign LORD is on me, because the LORD has anointed me to preach good news to the poor. He has sent me to bind up the brokenhearted, to proclaim freedom for the captives and release from darkness for the prisoners, to proclaim the year of the LORD's favor and the day of vengeance for our God, to comfort all who mourn, and provide for those who grieve in Zion — to bestow on them a crown of beauty instead of ashes, the oil of gladness instead of mourning, and a garment of praise instead of a spirit of despair. (Isaiah 61:–3)

The following story graphically illustrates the message of Isaiah 61:1-3.

Prasad was only ten when sold into slavery. His mother didn't want to do it, but she had no choice. His father, an alcoholic, left the family destitute having squandered all his salary on booze, much like many of the poor men in the rural, Indian villages. (Alcoholism among the poor in the slums of India is widespread and constitutes one of India's great social problems.) This father's guilt over his failure to provide for his family drove him to drink and thus use up the little money that could have been used to care for them. The hopelessness and dreariness of his life imprisoned him in despair far more effectively than any prison bars could ever have done. The result of all of it was the sale of Prasad as a bondslave to the local landowner.

He had two sons, and his younger son fell into a bonfire and was severely burned. He was away drunk when it happened. The little boy's mother had no money to get the necessary medical attention. She needed 125 rupees, and so she was driven to do the unthinkable, namely to sell her older son Prasad to the local landlord as a slave. With great sadness she went with

Prasad to the big home of the landlord and after haggling, put her thumbprint on a paper, signing her son's freedom away for 125 rupees (about $4.00).

As soon as the boy's mother disappeared, the landlord began to beat Prasad with a whip to make certain he understood he was a slave. Prasad became the landlord's shepherd, living among the wealthy man's sheep and sleeping in the sheep pen at night. He had barely enough to eat.

One day two of his friends approached him and invited him to attend a Children's Bible Club meeting. Prasad was interested and the following day he convinced an old man to watch the sheep while he went to the club meeting. He was thrilled with the action songs, but was especially thrilled to hear about a God named Jesus who could set us free. He was so interested that he forgot all about the old man and the sheep. When he did return, all the sheep had run away. It took him several hours to round them up; and the landlord, upon finding out what he had done, beat him mercilessly.

In spite of the beating Prasad was determined to find out more about this Jesus who set people free, and so once again, the following morning, he went back to the club meeting, and while there his sheep disappeared again. The same thing happened upon his return home after gathering his sheep: the landlord beat him until he started to bleed. That night, unable to sleep because of visions of Jesus, Prasad knelt and prayed to this God Jesus to be set free.

The next day he again went to the club and when the leader saw how beat up he was, he asked what had happened. Prasad told them that his mother had sold him as a slave to get money for medicine to save the life of his little brother, and that the landlord who owned him was beating him for coming to the Bible club.

The other kids gathered around Prasad and prayed that God would set him free. The teacher contacted the pastor of the Indian church that was sponsoring the Children's Bible Club and told him the story. That Sunday the little Indian church, in spite of its poverty, raised enough money in a collection to buy Prasad back from the landlord. Since Prasad was continually losing the sheep, the landlord was very happy to get his money refunded.

Everything Isaiah predicted in 61:1–3 now came true in Prasad's life. He was set free from being the landlord's slave; but more, he was set free from his sin to a life of freedom with Jesus. The ashes of sorrow and darkness turned into a crown of beauty on his head. He led his mother and younger brother to Christ and eventually his father as well. He then went on to become a teacher in the Children's Bible Club program and led many other boys and girls to Christ.

Prasad was set free because someone gave one dollar to Mission India, enabling him to go to a ten-day Children's Bible Club. This is the cost of giving a child in India thirty hours of exposure to the Bible, the love of a Christian teacher and a believing community, the power of prayer, action songs and games. That single dollar enabled not only Prasad to come to Jesus but also his mother and brother and his father, and the additional children that Prasad eventually taught in his own Children's Bible Clubs.

The one-dollar gift God used to set Prasad free started a tremendous river of freedom through which one person after another was set free. That one dollar was used to bring Prasad to the Lord, but can you imagine how many others as well, not just while Prasad lives but in the years that follow? Only Jesus sees the extent of the fulfillment of Isaiah's prophecy over and over and over. It is my hope and prayer when all of us get to heaven we will be able to see down those massive Mississippi-like rivers that flowed from our lives every time we gave to bring others to Christ.

REFLECTION AND DISCUSSION

1. What impressed you the most in this story?
2. Have you ever seen your gifts multiplied? How? When?

God Blesses Rice Bags

As he looked up, Jesus saw the rich putting their gifts into the temple treasury. He also saw a poor widow put in two very small copper coins. "I tell you the truth," he said, "this poor widow has put in more than all the others. All these people gave their gifts out of their wealth; but she out of her poverty put in all she had to live on." (Luke 21:1–4)

Jesus tells us through this incident, which we studied on day 21, that the true measure of the gift is not the amount but the proportion of the person's wealth that is given. The amount the widow gave was insignificant, but the proportion of her gift compared to her income was far beyond the proportion of the gift of the wealthy people.

I have always been impressed by the ways poor Indian Christian families find to give when they have barely enough to live on. One of the ways they give is by saving rice each day in a little bag—a rice bag. Each evening when the mother makes the evening meal, she carefully measures out a handful of rice for each family member and a final handful of rice for Jesus. Many of these poor families have little cloth bags into which they pour this rice each day and then bring it to church as their offering, pouring it into a large container. I wonder how Christ compares those rice-bag offerings of the poor in India with the average 2.5 percent of our income, which we in the West give to charity each year.

During the nineties I decided to challenge youth and children to follow the example of the poor Indian Christians by saving loose change in little rice bags and then giving it to Mission India to sponsor a person in a literacy class for $30. Wherever I introduced it, the kids responded overwhelmingly. One inner city Christian school in Texas encouraged their students to give their lunch money to India and provided a "free" lunch for all those who gave.

A large homeschooling curriculum company decided to challenge their home-schoolers to save loose change for eight weeks in Mission India rice bags by promising that they would match whatever the children gave, up to $100,000. To the customers who signed up, Mission India sent out rice bags along with a video about literacy and encouraged the students to learn about the mission challenge in India and to save loose change for eight weeks to sponsor a person like Selvi.

As I read some of the stories the children shared about their experiences in giving their "widow's mite" I wept for joy. These stories were among the most rewarding that I have ever read. The homeschoolers, like all children, plunged in with creative ideas that far exceeded merely gathering loose change. Here are a few of the stories.

From one family: "Today is my daughter's 6th birthday. . . . When we received the information about the literacy program in India, she was flabbergasted as to how someone could not be able to read. The video reduced her to tears. At her urging we sent rice bags to her friends to fill with change in lieu of traditional gifts for her birthday party and everyone was delighted to comply. Her party ended a few hours ago and we tallied the loose change: $82.00. It included 1,000 pennies. She is so excited to send her birthday gift to help bring literacy to women in India."

From a family in Florida: "Our daughters saved coins, collected birthday money, and filled up our coin jar. We also had a deal that every memory verse they learned would earn $2 each, so we made our goal of $600 before week eight."

From a family in Minnesota: "My seven wonderful children emptied their piggy banks to raise money. When they told Grandpa, he said he would match them if they could reach their goal of $100. Well, they got to $105 and Grandpa matched them and then Sonlight matched the total for a gift of $420."

From another family: "Our two boys

started their rice bag project by collecting every bit of loose change stored in our house, and it wasn't long before they ran out of loose change to collect. The boys then decided to make crafts and sell them from door to door. They spent hours and hours in their room making necklaces and canisters and pearl bead creations and sun catchers. They made over one hundred different items. They also saved money by sharing a drink rather than each buying one and skipping eating fast food and putting the money in the rice bag."

Many more of these stories poured in as we realized that God was teaching boys and girls to give while meeting the need for funds to bring literacy to people like Selvi in India. Our children are so responsive and teachable when it comes to giving and learning the multiplying lessons of saving by collecting loose change. The experience of God's marvelous multiplication is one of the most profound lessons we can teach them. Just as Christ commented on the widow's mite, saying that she gave more than all the others, I wonder if the same blessed words were said over these precious little ones who have given so much in proportion to their income.

REFLECTION AND DISCUSSION

1. In what ways are you teaching children to give?
2. While we react to the size of the gift, God blesses the "cost" of the gift. What is your giving "costing"?
3. Discuss the potential impact of not teaching the next generation to give sacrificially.

Biblical Giving Results in Joy

This final week of meditations is based on 2 Corinthians 8:1–7. Joy and giving cannot be separated, according to Paul. He uses the generosity of the poorest church among all the churches of that time as an example. Here is a summary of the seven ways in which giving leads to joy.

1. The joy of giving comes from being like God. God's nature is giving. To give is the very essence of his being. To be created in the image of God means that we have a choice to use this God-likeness of giving or we can deny that image and live for ourselves. To give is the gift God gives us when he made us in his likeness and through it allows us to share his eternal joy.

2. The joy of giving starts in sympathy for

others. He uses two drilling bits; the drill bit of trials and the drill bit of extreme poverty. Through these he sensitizes us to the needs of others, and that new sensitivity results in rich generosity and overflowing joy.

3. *The joy of giving is in discovering infinite resources.* Our giving is never limited to our resources, but true giving always exceeds our means. While it is important that we live sensibly, within our means, God expects us to give in faith and trust that he will supply what we need to give. When we live with enough we can then give in abundance.

4. *The joy of giving comes from within.* Motivation for giving does not come from emotional appeals about human need. It is not based on clever advertising manipulation. Giving is driven from the inner urge of God's Spirit, convincing us to give. That inner urge is the joy of the Lord (Nehemiah 8:10).

5. *The joy of giving comes from Christ's example.* Our giving is motivated not first by human needs but first by looking at the sacrifice of Christ, who dwells in us, and

whose presence makes our entire being glow with love and generosity. It was the "joy that was set before him" that enabled him to endure the cross (Hebrews 12:2).

6. *The joy of giving comes from motivating others to give.* We should stimulate each other to systematic and organized giving and hold up the generosity of the poor to encourage all to give.

7. *God's grace produces giving and giving produces joy.* Just as we excel in all virtues and rejoice in that excellence so we are to excel in the "grace of giving."

The Joy of Giving Comes from Being Like God

Now I want you to know, dear brothers and sisters, what God in his kindness had done through the churches in Macedonia. (2 Corinthians 8:1 NLT)

Whoever believes in me, as the Scripture has said, streams of living water will flow from within him." By this he meant the Spirit, whom those who believed in him were later to receive. Up to that time the Spirit had not been given, since Jesus had not yet been glorified. (John 7:38–39)

To be able to give is God's gift to us. Perhaps that sounds confusing, but that is how Paul starts 2 Corinthians 8 and 9, which is a two-chapter discourse on giving. (Incidentally, these two chapters are the longest discourse on giving in the Bible.) He says that the poorest of the New Testament churches was selected by God for a special treasure, the treasure of being able to give. Paul calls this the "grace of giving." Many of us approach giving as if we are helping out a God who is poverty stricken and cannot provide resources enough for his causes. He needs our help! God does not need our money, because he has it already! We are stewards of *his* money. We don't own anything!

Paul introduces the subject of giving as something that God did for the poor Macedonian churches, not something they did for him. Their giving is the result of God's grace shown to them. Our ability to give is a supernatural treasure of God's grace, to be cherished and held up as an example of God's gift to us. When we give, we are in reality accepting God's treasure of joy that he gives to us. Each time we give we take God's gift of joy.

S. Martin wrote a story called "The Richest Family in Church." It is about a poor family, consisting of a widowed mom and her three daughters, sixteen, fourteen, and twelve. It takes place in the Easter Season of 1946. The pastor of their little church of eighty had announced that on Easter they would take an offering for a very poor family. He asked all to save during the month and then give sacrificially on Easter Sunday. The offering would be taken to the poor family on Easter Sunday afternoon.

When the widow and the girls got home they were excited about what they could do to help that poor family. They scrimped and saved, eating only potatoes, turning off the lights more frequently, and not listening to the radio. They got house-cleaning jobs and did yard work. They made pot holders, which they sold. That month of sacrificing and saving was the best, most enjoyable month of their lives.

They talked about how much they were saving each day, and they would sit in the dark on their beds anticipating how much the poor family would enjoy having all the money the church would give. God's grace was at work in their lives creating the joy of giving, as they committed themselves to saving money to give to the mysterious poor family. They figured that the church probably could give twenty times what they were raising since everyone else had so much more than they did. By Easter they had saved $70. They felt like millionaires. Each of the girls carefully placed a new $20 bill in the offering plate and Mom topped it off with her new $10 bill. They celebrated that noon as they ate their Easter dinner of fried potatoes and boiled eggs.

Late that afternoon the pastor came to their home with an envelope, which he gave to the mother, and after a few words, left. The daughters gathered around the table, curious about the strange envelope. They opened it and to their amazement three new $20 bills, one new $10 bill and seventeen $1 bills fell out. They were the poor family and they had given $70, while the entire rest of the church had given only $17.

One of the daughters recounts, "That Easter day I found out we were poor. The minister had brought us the money for the poor family, so we must be poor. I didn't like being poor. I looked at my dress and worn-out shoes and felt so ashamed—I didn't even want to go back to church. . . . We sat in silence for a long time. Then it got dark, and we went to bed. All that week . . . no one talked much. What did poor people do with money? We didn't know. We'd never known we were poor. We went from such excitement and joy to the pits of sadness. We didn't want to go to church that next Sunday, but Mom said we had to. . . . At church we had a missionary speak. He talked about how their church in Africa made a new building out of sun-dried bricks, but they needed money to buy the roof. He said $100 would put a roof on their church. The minister said, 'Can't we all sacrifice to help these poor people?'

"We looked at each other and smiled for the first time that week. Mom reached into her purse and pulled out the envelope with the $70 and the $17 one-dollar bills. She passed it to Darlene, and Darlene gave it to me, and I passed it to Ocy. Ocy put it in the offering. When the offering was counted, the minister announced that it was a little over $100. *We were the rich family in the church!* Hadn't the missionary said so? From that day on I've never been poor again! Oh, how we love to give. It brings such joy!"

The mom and her three daughters were like the Macedonian church: recipients of the "grace of giving," the most prized treasure in God's infinite treasury. The poor family's gift came from joy. The gift of the church came from guilt. I don't know if the story is true, but the pattern certainly is true. True giving is joyful; it is entering into the "joy of the Lord."

When we take Western Christians to India they all return with the same response—they have never seen such an incredible level of joy. That joy comes from sacrificial giving. It is sacrificial giving without realizing the sacrifice. True giving is the giving of the three girls and their mom, of the poor Macedonian church, and of the precious little homeschool kids who did the rice-bag projects. God's grace of giving is never a little flippant tip to God for good service; it is a significant, costly offering expressing profound love.

REFLECTION AND DISCUSSION

1. Why did the poor family enjoy giving so much and feel dignified through it?
2. Can you share a story from personal experience illustrating God's work of giving through those who don't have much?

The Joy of Giving Begins in Sympathy for Others

Out of the most severe trial, their overflowing joy and their extreme poverty welled up in rich generosity. (2 Corinthians 8:2)

On that day a great persecution broke out against the church at Jerusalem, and all except the apostles were scattered throughout Judea and Samaria. . . . Those who had been scattered preached the word wherever they went. (Acts 8:1, 4)

Blessed are you when people insult you, persecute you and falsely say all kinds of evil against you because of me. Rejoice

and be glad, because great is your
reward in heaven, for in the same way
they persecuted the prophets who were
before you. (Matthew 5:11–12)

I was riding with a Mission India colleague in the valley of central California, and I had been grumbling unabatedly. In his weariness of hearing my incessant complaints, he said, "John. Look at those mountains. They are beautiful, aren't they?" I had to agree but didn't know what he was getting at. "How many tomatoes are grown on those mountain peaks?" he continued. "Obviously farming isn't the best up there, is it? Look at the tomato fields down here in the valley. These valleys in California are amazingly fertile.

"You are in a spiritual valley right now and you are grumbling and complaining about everything. Don't you realize that as much as you want to live on the mountaintops, precious little fruit is grown there? Spiritual fruit, like natural fruit, is generally grown in the valleys of life, not on the mountaintops."

The Macedonian church had experienced two horrible valleys—one of extreme trial and the other of extreme poverty. Paul says that it was in these two valleys that the rich fruit of overwhelming generosity flourished and brought about abundant joy and created sympathy for others going through similar problems.

As I write this I think of Jim Franks, founder of International Aid, who brought hundreds of container loads of used hospital equipment to little, poor hospitals in rural China. I remember his story of the Chinese elder who was puzzled by the huge load of good, but used, medical equipment. He could not believe it when Jim told him that the equipment was "outdated" and would be thrown away, since it was replaced by new equipment. The Chinese elder's face grew dark as he said, "Oh, Brother Jim, we must pray for you! How can you possibly see Jesus when you have so many material things blocking your vision? We do not have that problem here in China. We can see Jesus directly, since we are so poor. No material goods stand in our way."

Was it the combination of a hard trial and extreme poverty that penetrated the Macedonian church and softened them to be sympathetic, motivating them to give? God uses trial and persecution to break our selfishness and move us to give to the poor and fatherless.

The hundreds and hundreds of people we have taken to see the work in India over the past 30 years are always amazed at the joy of the Indian believers in the midst of some of the worst poverty on earth. Their joy is so much greater than any joy we experience in the affluent West. A Christian leader in the Philippines answered my question concerning the welfare of his denomination by saying, "It is wonderful. Twelve pastors were martyred this year." He went on to explain, "Persecution cleanses and resets our faces toward God. Through persecution we are seeing eternal values."

Peter's words affirm this function of trials, poverty, and persecution:

These have come so that your faith— of greater worth than gold, which perishes even though refined by fire — may be proved genuine and may result in praise, glory and honor when Jesus Christ is revealed. Though you have not seen him, you love him; and even though you do not see him now, you believe in him and are filled with an inexpressible and glorious joy for you are receiving the goal of your faith, the salvation of your souls. (1 Peter 1:7–9)

Jacob, one of Mission India's workers, hails from the southern state of Kerala and works in the northern state of Assam. He was captured by a gang of terrorists and accused of unlawfully converting people to Christianity as a foreigner. The gang surrounded him with rifles ready to shoot. The chief of the terrorists gave him a shovel and told him to dig his grave six feet deep so he could stand in it. They wanted to bury him standing up! Jacob dug until his head was below the surface of the ground. The terrorists pulled him up and stood him on the edge of the hole.

As he stood, waiting for the chief to

command his men to shoot, he prayed. "Jesus, I have a little girl at home, and I have much work to do here. I am not ready yet to come home to you. I will submit to your will, but I ask that your will be that I am spared." His eyes filled with tears as he told me that the next two minutes seemed like an eternity as the powerful presence of Christ descended upon the group. It was as if they could feel Jesus there, protecting his servant. Suddenly the chief commanded the men to lower their rifles and all turned and disappeared into the bushes, leaving Jacob standing by the open grave.

As he related this experience, his demeanor changed to pure joy, inexpressible joy! It was a radiant joy that everyone listening could feel as he said that he never, ever again would doubt his Savior, and through this extreme trial and persecution, his faith was tested and strengthened. The power he felt in those moments would propel him in giving for the rest of his life.

As trials descend on us and unexpected financial strain leaves us sleepless at night, we must be aware that God is drilling holes in the hard pan of our materialism to allow the joy, the life-giving Spirit, to gush out of us. We need to have our eyes lifted from our worship of the "idol of material possessions" to eternal values. That is a most painful process but a most important experience. Not only do the trials make us see eternal values but give to us the sensitivity needed to allow God to use us as channels of his infinite resources in ministering to the needs of others.

REFLECTION AND DISCUSSION

1. What trials and persecutions have you endured, and what has been their impact on your faith and sensitivity to others?
2. What impressed you the most in this meditation? Why?

The Joy of Giving Is in Discovering Infinite Resources

For I testify that they gave as much as they were able, and even beyond their ability. (2 Corinthians 8:3)

Now to Him who is able to do exceedingly abundantly above all that we ask or think. (Ephesians 3:20)

We are to give beyond our ability to give. This is a profound lesson that all Christians need to learn. *We must live within our means but give beyond our means.* Remember the young people we heard about on day 25? They took up the challenge to raise $10,000 in 1967, and raised $12,500, learning this lesson in a profound way. They gave beyond their ability, and it startled them, their parents, and the entire church. It filled the whole congregation with a sense of joy few other experiences could have provided. We give out of God's resources, not our own; and when the need is legitimate, God will supply. This supplying will be done using means that reflect his power and wealth, not human wealth and power.

Oswald Chambers, in his book *My Utmost for His Highest*, warns about the dangers of common sense. Common sense always points to human intelligence and away from God. When things reflect common sense, humans are elevated, not God. God calls us to give beyond our means, beyond common sense, as did the Macedonian church.

I challenged the students in a chapel service at a local Christian college to ask God to give them $20 over and above what they had at that moment in order to give that $20 to Mission India. The $20 had to be money that came to them in some unusual way. It could not be money they had at the present time, but unexpected money. Students don't have much money. The challenge to ask God to give them an extra $20 for missions was significant. They had to step out in faith and prayer.

A number of students sent in $20, but it was not until many years later that I discovered a most remarkable story. After I spoke at a mission conference a young man came up to me and excitedly asked if I remembered challenging the student body at that Christian college. He said that his entire attitude toward giving had been dramatically changed by the message. He prayed that God would give him $20. During the course of the week his friend asked him to take care of the gym for just one morning and gave him $20 for his work. He spent it. The following Sunday, as he prayed for $20, he realized that God had given it to him and he "blew it." So he prayed again that God would provide him with $20 in a very special way.

During the second week another friend asked him if he remembered loaning him

$20 about four years earlier. He said he had totally forgotten about it. The friend confessed that he too had forgotten to pay him back but for some strange reason had been prompted that week to repay the loan. He gave him an unexpected $20, saying the time had come to pay up. The young man, startled at the windfall, took the money and feeling flush, spent it, only to realize again on Sunday when he prayed for $20 that God had already given him an unexpected $20 a second time.

On the third Sunday he confessed his stupidity in not seeing how God had answered his prayers and prayed one more time for $20. This time, however, he asked God to give him $20 in such a way that he would not miss it. He asked that it be given in a startling, unexpected way. It was his birthday that week and he received a birthday card from a friend who had never acknowledged his birthday before, and in it was a $20 bill. This time he recognized God's hand and sent the funds on to Mission India.

He told me that the experience, which sounds too strange to be true, had totally transformed his concept of giving. He understood that what he gave came from God. He had nothing to give. From that day on he responded to the challenge to give in the light of God's resources, not his! His giving was motivated by what God wanted to give through him, not by what he had. He practiced "faith promise giving" ever since, pledging to give to God whatever excess God gave to him in unusual ways. His life as a Christian had been exciting and joy filled.

In 2 Corinthians 9:8, Paul tells the Corinthians, "And God is able to make all grace abound to you, so that in all things at all times, having all that you need, you will abound in every good work." The "prosperity gospel" has it all wrong. God never promises us that we can live in abundance and then give enough. He promises us that he will give us all that we need so that we can *give in abundance. The promise is not that we live in abundance but that we give in abundance.*

Think of two triangles. One rests upside down, on its point, and rises up to spread out. The other is in the normal position, like a pyramid, with the point on the top. Biblical giving is like the first triangle with the point on the bottom and the lines going up, spreading out. God will always give us enough to live on so that we can give in abundance. He never promises us that we can live in abundance, only that we can give in abundance! Our giving most often resembles the opposite—the spreading part of the triangle represents what we own and the tip what we give.

Can God say that you are giving beyond your ability? Too often we slip into living beyond our means. That spells trouble. Giving beyond our means, however, is the doorway to miracles and joy.

REFLECTION AND DISCUSSION

1. Have you had unusual experiences in which God supplied unexpected funds for your giving?
2. Are you willing to try asking God for a specific amount of money, for a cause close to your heart, given during a month's time, like the young man in this meditation? Try it!

DAY 32

The Joy of Giving Comes from Within

Entirely on their own, they urgently pleaded with us for the privilege of sharing in this service for the saints.
(2 Corinthians 8:3–4)

It was dark, and I had promised the weary group I would have them back at the hotel before dark. At 6:30 I was ready to load the tour group on the bus and forget about the meeting. I was furious, but the project manager for the literacy class begged me to wait just "two minutes" more, the typical Indian euphemism for an indeterminate deadline. And so we waited.

Finally, at 6:45, the thirty students showed up, all women and all dressed like the Queen of Sheba. They were beautiful. They had on their best saris and jewelry. Their faces were powdered and each of them had flowers in her hair.

"See," the project manager said with a great grin on his face, "before they learned to read they would have come right out of the fields where they worked all day, smelling of sweat and dirt. They have been taught all their life that they are subhuman, less than cows. They had no dignity, no self-image. But now, since you have enabled them to read and write and told them about Jesus, they know that they have been created in God's image and are important. They are so important that they could not come to see you without bathing, putting on their best clothes, and putting flowers in their hair. You have given them the gift of dignity."

I stood there with tears flowing down my cheeks, overwhelmed (and fairly shamed) at the beautiful transformation brought by Christ through the dignity of literacy. That first instance, thirty years ago, of seeing the profound effect of literacy hooked me. My joy in seeing the results of literacy in the beauty of the women in this class was unforgettable. To see people who were taught that they were subhuman stand before us with flowers in their hair, reading their primers to us, brought all of us to tears of joy.

Paul's description of the Macedonian Christians in this verse was exactly what happened to me. There are six important concepts in this little verse that describe God's glorifying giving.

1. "Entirely on their own . . ." The Macedonians were not responding to some high-pressure pitch or some clever manipulation. Nor was I. It was a genuine, heart-moving transformation to see these women. True giving is born out of the Spirit's testimony in our hearts concerning the unique way he wishes each of us to become a river of life. We must be careful never to manipulate others to give, but always to allow room for them to "give on their own" in direct response to the personal

prompting of the Holy Spirit.

2. "They urgently . . ." This prompting of the Holy Spirit always has an urgency about it. We need passion in our giving, a passion that drives us to give beyond our means and ability and motivates us to trust God to supply our resources in supernatural and unexpected ways. Giving must never be grudging, for that kind of giving will never introduce us to the eternal joy of giving. As Christ faced the cross, kneeling in the garden, sweating drops of blood, there obviously was an urgency burning in his soul, knowing the salvation of the world rested upon those moments.

3. "Pleaded . . ." This is an interesting description of giving — pleading to give! This is God-glorifying giving. How often we see this pleading to give in times of natural disaster. In 2005 Hurricane Katrina brought that kind of response from the Christian community throughout America. Much of the relief work

was done by Christians pleading to help, while the government
agencies wallowed in bureaucratic
nightmares of inefficiency.

4. "With us for the privilege . . ."
Giving is a privilege, and those
who give regularly are well aware
of it. Jesus summed it up: "It
is more blessed to give than to
receive" (Acts 20:35) is experienced
time and again in the tremendous
joy that flows from generosity. Life
finds meaning and purpose in the
transformation of others through
giving.

5. "Of sharing . . ." The deepest
and most wonderful compliment
that can be given is the statement, "I don't know what I would
have done without you." Sharing
in one another's burdens is the
cement binding us together in
God-glorifying community. All of
us long for the kind of friends who
fit that statement.

6. "In this service for the saints . . ."
Giving is service. We have been

given new life as God's gift of pure
grace, for the purpose of doing
good works, which God planned
for us even before we were born
(Ephesians 2:10). Those good works
are service to others in Christ's
name and bring joy both to those
served and the servers.

God's Spirit works in us, motivating
us to give, entirely on our own without
human manipulation, as he brings needs
to our attention that are uniquely fitted to
our positions of meeting them.

REFLECTION AND DISCUSSION

1. What are the needs that move you to
   give "entirely on your own"?
2. Describe the times you felt an "urgent
   need" to give.
3. How important is it to reflect on the
   results of your giving? If you fail to
   do this, do you miss some of the joy of
   giving? Explain.

The Joy of Giving Comes from Christ's Example

And they did not do as we expected, but they gave themselves first to the Lord and then to us in keeping with God's will. (2 Corinthians 8:5)

In this short verse we find the ultimate motivation for giving, the ultimate result of giving, and the ultimate method of giving. Motivation for giving comes from looking at Christ's gift on the cross. The greatest missionary force in modern times was the Moravian missionaries, who were driven by their motto, "Worthy is the Lamb to receive his reward!" When driven by the motivation of gratitude for Christ's sacrifice we can expect unexpected results, such as Paul saw in the Macedonian Christians' gift. One could not expect a gift of such magnitude given their poor circumstances. Because it was motivated by gratitude for Christ's gift and given in ways beyond human explanation it was a gift that was given according to God's way of giving ... and thus produced in the Macedonian church an exceptional experience of divine joy.

Cluttered vision is one of the primary hindrances to giving. Our minds are cluttered with desires for material things. If it is not the desire of getting some possession that keeps us from seeing Jesus, it is then the anxiety of losing some possession.

I think of the tribal husband in India who, upon finding that Jesus had cured his wife from a lifelong illness, took all the ugly idol gods out of the house and smashed them in the courtyard. He declared that from then on they would look only at the beauty of Jesus.

What this tribal man did both literally and spiritually is exactly what we Western Christians need to do. God has entrusted us, though representing only 30 percent of the Christians in the world, with 85 percent of all Christian wealth, according to statistics in David Barrett's *Encyclopedia of World Christianity*. We are the bankers of world Christianity, but it seems that we are caught in a credit crunch and are not the enablers and givers we should be, as I pointed out earlier. We are looking at money, programs, and our buildings, rather than at the Savior. When we focus on the Savior and his gift on Calvary as did the Macedonian Christians, we will be filled with an awe and wonder that washes away the love of transient toys. The river cleanses the passion to acquire them, along with the anxiety of losing them.

Leslie Weatherhead, in *The Transforming Friendship*, captures this wonder at Jesus in the story of a vision in which he sees a man walking past a little house on Christmas Eve. Looking in the window the man saw four children arguing in the front room, while in the kitchen a harried single mother attempted to make the celebration of Christmas a joyous affair. As the man looked on, he saw Christ enter, walk into the front room, and get down on his knees and play with the children. At bedtime, he quietly led them upstairs, tucked them in, and then came down to the kitchen and sat at the table.

The housewife, without looking at him, kept up her frantic preparation for the Christmas meal the next day. As she worked, she poured out one complaint after another: Her husband had deserted her, she had no money for toys, and her future was insecure and bleak. Complaint after complaint and problem after problem poured from her lips. Finally she too sat down, but the complaints continued.

Slowly, the Savior reached across the table and gently touched her chin, lifting her face until her eyes met his. In that glorious moment all her complaints and questions stopped. They didn't matter any longer. As she beheld his beauty, tenderness, love, and peace, nothing seemed important. She wanted to look at him forever.

When we divorce giving from looking at Jesus and give only on the basis of human need, we lose the primary motivation of love and gratitude for Christ's unfathomable gift. If the human need of India were the primary reason for giving, I would have gone crazy years ago. I am driven to give to the Lord for India not because it is the most needy nation but because of the infinite love and sacrifice of our Savior on the cross. It is only by giving first to the Lord that I can then continue in positive joy in giving to the saints in need in India.

REFLECTION AND DISCUSSION

1. What were some of the most awesome spiritual experiences of your life, especially in reflecting on Christ's dying for you on Calvary?
2. What was the most valuable lesson you learned from this meditation?

The Joy of Giving Comes from Motivating Others to Give

So we have urged Titus, who encouraged your giving in the first place, to return to you and encourage you to finish this ministry of giving. (2 Corinthians 8:6 NLT)

[Jesus said,] "Be careful not to do your 'acts of righteousness' before men, to be seen by them. If you do, you will have no reward from your Father in heaven. So when you give to the needy, do not announce it with trumpets, as the hypocrites do in the synagogues and on

the streets, to be honored by men. I tell you the truth, they have received their reward in full." (Matthew 6:1–2)

When Christ told us to give secretly, he was speaking about our motivation for giving. He was not saying all giving should be secret, for if that is what he meant, then Paul—though inspired of God—would somehow be wrong in holding up the Macedonians' giving as an example for all. When we are motivated to give because of the honor others give us, then we had best give secretly. However, when we give out of love for Jesus and give as the Macedonian Christians gave, our example of giving may be shared to encourage others. Paul sent Titus to the Corinthian church to complete the giving that was started but evidently had lagged behind. He rightfully used the example of the poor Macedonians to spur them on to giving more. We must spur each other on through examples of giving, making certain that we are not glorifying humans but pointing to Christ.

Brother Daniel, an Indian evangelist, came to us several years ago with a unique plan and request. He wanted to distribute 250,000 packets containing a Bible course, a gospel and two tracts to 250,000 homes, reaching two million people in India. The cost would be $160,000. He went on to explain the origin of this plan.

He explained that he had fifteen churches making this request. They were growing rapidly, and hundreds of Hindus were coming to Christ. A few months earlier, the churches underwent a severe attack by terrorists. The terrorists came into one of the villages, grabbed a young man who had recently begun to follow Jesus, and told him to recant, proclaiming India was a Hindu nation and not a Christian nation. They said they would kill him if he refused. He refused. Immediately they cut off his nose. He continued to refuse. They cut out his tongue and then completed his murder by hacking him to pieces as a warning to the churches that if they did not stop their witnessing this would happen to many more people.

Daniel went on to say that that young man's death, rather than inspiring fear, increased the Indian Christians' resolve. It was in his honor that this plan to distribute that immense amount of Scripture was designed. We shared that story with a group of businessmen here in the United States and asked them to help raise the $160,000.

Late that night, one of the businessmen called me. He was a young man and a close friend. He had been informed by doctors that he had only a short time to live because of cancer. His father had died of cancer and he had a brother dying of cancer, and now it seemed it was his turn. But God had other plans for him, and after a prayer meeting at our church with our elders, this man had been totally and miraculously healed. He called that night to tell me that he could not sleep. He wanted to give the entire $160,000.

A couple of months later I called on him personally and gave him an opportunity to get out of his pledge, telling him that the day had been pretty emotional and that he perhaps had made that pledge without realizing the real cost.

Tears of joy streamed down his face as he responded to my words. "John, do you know what has happened? A few weeks after I made that pledge, the treasurer of my factory came into my office and told me that we had a very unusual year last year. There were no claims against workers' compensation insurance. This resulted in a rebate check, which he then laid on my desk. It was in the amount of $171,000!

I often shared this story in my preaching, and in one of those churches a paraplegic veteran sat in a wheelchair, in the middle aisle of the church, completely caught up in the story. I didn't get a chance to meet him that night, but about a month later I received a letter from his pastor containing a check for $500 made out for Mission India. The pastor told me that the man was one of the poorest people in his church but had just been awarded a settlement by the government for his injuries in Vietnam. It was a meager sum of only $5,000, almost an insult for what he had endured. But the paraplegic veteran was so inspired by the businessman that he wanted to give 10 percent of the tiny settlement to the Lord!

Before I left the pastorate to devote myself fulltime to serving the Lord for India, I had a most unusual congregation who loved giving to missions. This church had introduced faith-promise giving to our denomination by their example, and their giving was about $42,000 per year in 1977 when I first came. I remember those exciting services each year when the people would pledge their faith promises for the coming twelve months and then wait as the deacons tallied up the total. How they clapped with excitement as the total rose dramatically year after year, from $42,000 to $127,000 in just four years' time. They had the joy of motivating each other to give.

We must encourage each other to new heights of giving and, as Titus was commissioned to do, carry out that which we pledge to do.

REFLECTION AND DISCUSSION

1. How have you been inspired by the generosity of others?
2. What moved you the most in this meditation?

The Joy of Giving
Is the Joy of
Christian Virtues

Since you excel in so many ways—in your faith, your gifted speakers, your knowledge, your enthusiasm, and your love from us—I want you to excel also in this gracious act of giving.
(2 Corinthians 8:7 NLT)

I want to conclude this week's meditation by quoting part of a field report written by Dr. Donald Chapman, Mission India's vice president of ministry:

"Just over 100 years ago, the Mizo people (in northeast India) were headhunters. Then in 1894, missionaries from Wales were sent there by a rich business-man to evangelize these people. I can't imagine the faith of those missionaries as they risked their lives. What true heroes and servants of Christ. Within 50 years, the entire Mizo people became follow-ers of Jesus. Today there are 900,000 Mizo people and 99 percent are Christians. It is not just peer pressure and conformity that guides these people. God has planted a mission vision in their hearts. One of every 500 Mizo people is a missionary. Most are sent to other areas in India, but they have a growing international presence as well. The Chief Minister of this state has publicly announced his goal of Mizoram sending out 100,000 missionaries!

"The churches in Mizoram meet three times every Sunday: morning, afternoon, and evening. There are also services every Wednesday and Saturday evening. [I attended] a Sunday morning service, and as we walked into the lobby area, there was a huge aluminum kettle, perhaps three feet in diameter, in the center. As families would walk by, they poured the contents of plastic grocery sacks or round containers into this now nearly full vessel. Rice filled it. This Sunday church members brought rice as their contribution to the poor. This was not their weekly church offering, but rather another example of the habit of giving that graced every family in the church.

"After the service we visited several homes. I wanted to see and understand how this poor church in a tiny state in Northeast India could have so many full-time missionaries sent to other states in India. In the first home the lady of the house showed us a two-gallon plastic bucket. There was a label stuck on the outside. It read "The Lord's Share." At every meal the woman of the house sets aside a portion of rice considered "The Lord's Share" in this plastic bucket. It might be as small as a handful but much more depending on the financial status of the family. But in every home, at every meal, the Lord gets his share. Then on Saturday morning, volunteers collect the rice from each family. A woman volunteers for a month on Saturdays and visits each of ten to twelve homes assigned to her, records the amount the family gives in a ledger, and carries the rice on her back in a basket strapped around her forehead. She brings it to one of many collection points throughout the city. In the Presbyterian Church alone, more than five million kilograms of rice are collected each year. That is the equivalent of an annual gift of 5,500 tons of rice.

"The Mizoram church is a poor church considering that the average per capita income for the state is $150 per year. But it is a very generous church. Some of the rice is sold at 55 percent of its retail value to poor families and the funds are given to the church treasurer. Most of the church activities are funded by the rice through the disciplined regular giving of every family.

"In addition to funding church activities and feeding very poor people, the rice offering also supports 1,500 full-time missionaries sent out into India without any other support from outside Mizoram. Each family gives daily rice *in addition to tithing their income!* These people, living on an average income of only $150 a year, give 25 percent to the church; and the church in turn gives 46 percent of its income to finance missionaries to bring the gospel to others."

I believe the Mizoram Presbyterians are the Macedonian example of giving for today! It is our prayer that their example would spur our Western Christians to more sacrificial, regular, organized giving, encouraging each other by example to excel in the grace of giving!

REFLECTION AND DISCUSSION

1. What impressed you the most about the Mizoram Christians?
2. Why does it seem that the poor give proportionally more than the wealthy?
3. Discuss: All you have belongs to God. What you live on is your overhead. Thus, the real question is not how much you give but how much you keep for your administration.

"A Christmas Carol" ends with Ebenezer Scrooge dancing through the village, gleefully laughing, as he somewhat recklessly distributes gifts. The author, Charles Dickens, captured the joyful transformation from the slavery of getting to the freedom of giving.

Has this series of meditations helped you find that joy? Reflect in the remaining five days of this forty day period, on what you have learned during each of the five weeks.

From Week 1

We give because we are born again to be rivers, not lakes.

In what ways has the idea that you are born again to be a river, not a lake, affected your life?

From Week 2

We give the seven gifts of Christ.

What are those seven gifts of Christ?

To whom are you giving those seven gifts, and how are you giving them?

From Week 3

We give because, through our gifts, God gives gifts he would not give, had we not given.

What Scripture stories illustrating this truth impressed you?

How has your giving encouraged others to give?

What is the definition of discipleship in John 13:34–35, and how is that different than the commonly accepted definition?

From Week 4

We give because biblical giving enables others to give.

Have you committed to pray for a special gift from God to give to some cause, giving God an opportunity for you to experience how he can supply in unusual ways?

How much will God give when you give?

How has this concept affected your giving?

From Week 5

We give because biblical giving results in eternal joy.

What are some of the ways in which giving produces joy?

For further information about Mission India and its ministry, visit us online at www.missionindia.org, write to Mission India, PO Box 141312, Grand Rapids, MI 49514, or call (877) 644-6342.

Additional copies of both *Why Give?* and *Why Pray?* may be obtained from the above address.